FAITH AND FEMINISM

UNIVERSITY OF
WOLVERHAMPTON
KNOWLEDGE • INNOVATION • ENTERPRISE

Harrison Learning Centre
City Campus
University of Wolverhampton
St Peter's Square
Wolverhampton
WV1 1RH
Telephone: 0845 408 1631
Online renewals: www.wlv.ac.uk/lib/myaccount

Telephone Renewals: 01902 321333 or 0845 408 1631
Online Renewals: www.wlv.ac.uk/lib/myaccount
Please return this item on or before the last date shown above.
Fines will be charged if items are returned late.
See tariff of fines displayed at the Counter.

D1440558

Other titles in the series:

Shaping the Tools: Study Skills in Theology by Ruth Ackroyd and David Major

Choosing Life? Christianity and Moral Problems by Jeff Astley

God's World by Jeff Astley

Using the Bible: Studying the Text by Robert Evans

Communication and the Gospel by John Holdsworth

Literature in Christian Perspective: Becoming Faithful Readers by Bridget Nichols

Being Anglican by Alastair Redfern

Ministry and Priesthood by Alastair Redfern

God's Here and Now: Social Contexts of the Ministry of the People of God by Philip Richter

The Authority of the Bible by William Strange

Living Theology by Michael West, Graham Noble and Andrew Todd

EXPLORING
FAITH
Theology for Life

SERIES EDITORS: Leslie J Francis and Jeff Astley

FAITH AND FEMINISM

An Introduction to
Christian Feminist Theology

Nicola Slee

DARTON·LONGMAN+TODD

First published in 2003 by
Darton, Longman and Todd Ltd
1 Spencer Court
140-142 Wandsworth High Street
London SW18 4JJ

ISBN 0-232-52486-6

A catalogue record for this book is available from the British Library.

Designed by Sandie Boccacci
Phototypeset in Minion by Intype Libra Ltd
Printed and bound in Great Britain by
Page Bros, Norwich, Norfolk

CONTENTS

Preface   vii

Introduction   ix

1. Introduction to feminist theology: context and key
   concepts   1

2. Texts of terror or emancipatory discourse? The Bible in
   feminist perspective   13

3. What language shall I borrow? Religious language and
   models of God   25

4. Deadly innocence? Sin in feminist perspective   37

5. Can a male saviour save women? Christology in feminist
   perspective   48

6. Can redemption be redeemed? Salvation and atonement
   in feminist perspective   60

7. The Holy Spirit as the feminine in God? Pneumatology in
   feminist perspective   72

8. In search of a round table: ecclesiology in feminist
   perspective   83

9. The hope for wholeness: spirituality in feminist
   perspective   95

10. The future of feminist theology: gift and challenge to the
    churches   106

References   119

Glossary and biography   125

Index of themes   130

PREFACE

At the beginning of the third millennium a new mood is sweeping through the Christian churches. This mood is reflected in a more radical commitment to discipleship among a laity who wish to be theologically informed and fully equipped for Christian ministry in the secular world.

Exploring Faith: theology for life is designed for people who want to take Christian theology seriously in a way that engages the mind, involves the heart, and seeks active expression in the way we live. Those who explore their faith in this way are beginning to shape a theology for life.

Exploring Faith: theology for life is rooted in the individual experience of the world and in the ways through which God is made known in the world. Such experience is related to and interpreted in the light of the Christian tradition. Each volume is written by a scholar who has clear authority in the area of theology discussed and who takes seriously the ways in which busy adults learn. The series aims to open up key aspects of theology and explore these in dialogue with the readers' own experience.

The volumes are suitable for all those who wish to learn more about the Christian faith and ministry, including those who have already taken courses in Christian basics (such as *Alpha* and *Emmaus*) and have been inspired to undertake further study, those preparing to take theology as an undergraduate course, and those already engaged on certificate, diploma or degree programmes. The volumes have been developed for individuals to work on alone or for groups to study together.

Already groups of Christians are using the *Exploring Faith: theology for life* series throughout the United Kingdom, linked by exciting credit-bearing initiatives pioneered jointly by the churches and the academy. There are a number of ways in which learning Christians can find their way into award-bearing programmes through the series *Exploring Faith: theology for life*.

The series editors wish to express their personal thanks to colleagues who have helped them shape the series identity, especially Diane Drayson, Evelyn Jackson, Susan Thomas and Virginia Hearn, and to the individual authors who have produced high-quality text on schedule and so generously accepted firm editorial direction. The editorial work has been supported by the North of England Institute for Christian Education and the Welsh National Centre for Religious Education.

Leslie J Francis
Jeff Astley

INTRODUCTION

This book is intended as an introduction to, and an overview of, developments in feminist theology over the last three or four decades. When I first became interested in feminist theological ideas in the early eighties, it was quite possible to read and buy every book published in Britain in the field. I well remember the excitement of acquiring early texts such as Susan Dowell and Linda Hurcombe's *Dispossessed Daughters of Eve* (1981) and Sara Maitland's *A Map of the New Country* (1983). Today, only some twenty years later, the whole field of feminist theological studies has mushroomed exponentially into a vast, world-wide movement with many diverse perspectives, approaches and stances. It would be quite impossible for even the most dedicated scholar to read and acquire every significant text in even one limited area of the field, such as biblical studies, or from one specific country or context in which feminist theology is being conducted.

It may seem foolhardy, then, for anyone to attempt an overview of the field in a short text of this nature. Perhaps it is! Yet I regularly meet adults in the churches, women in the women's movement (if such a thing still exists), as well as theology students and ordinands (some of whom I teach) who have little formal knowledge of feminist theology yet who are curious to find out more about the key ideas of debate and the achievements of feminist theologians. I have written this text for them. It assumes no prior knowledge of feminist theology, though I imagine most readers will have picked up a general knowledge of the kinds of issues which feminist scholars have been exploring: for example, the question of God-language and whether and how we employ gendered language to speak of God, or the issue of how women can read an ancient patriarchal text such as the Bible as a meaningful word addressed to our lives today.

The text begins with a general introduction, which describes the emergence of feminist theology and identifies some of the key concepts employed by feminist theologians. Each of the succeeding chapters takes one key area of Christian theology and life – Bible, God-language, sin and the human condition, the person of Christ, redemption and atonement, the Holy Spirit, the Church and spirituality – and gives a survey, first of feminist critiques of traditional Christian understandings and then of constructive attempts by feminists to restate Christian doctrines and practices. The final chapter reviews and evaluates the achievements of feminist theology and looks to the future, asking what shape feminist theologies are likely to take. There are exercises throughout which can be done by an individual student or in a group setting. As well as questions for reflection and discussion, I have offered a number of more creative options such as creative writing and painting exercises, in the hope that this will enable students to enter more deeply and imaginatively into the challenges of feminist theology.

Clearly, it is impossible to be comprehensive in a text of this kind. What I have attempted to do is to sketch out broad trends in each chapter, identifying significant texts and thinkers, and showing something of the diversity of perspectives within feminist theological debate. On the whole, I have restricted my attention to *Christian* feminist theology, although I have also, from time to time, indicated the work of post-Christian or post-traditional theologians, particularly where it is offering trenchant critiques of Christian faith. The partiality and selectivity of the text of course reflects my own biases and location as a white, middle-class, privileged British woman. I hope, nevertheless, to have engaged sufficiently with a range of diverse perspectives for all readers to feel there are some points of contact in the text.

This text has taken shape out of my teaching over some twenty years in a number of learning institutions, as well as more informally in church settings and women's networks and groups. I should like to thank all my students who, over the years, have challenged me to engage afresh with feminist theological ideas and to find ways of enabling others to engage with them. At the time when I was beginning to be interested in feminist theology, I had no formal teachers, but I learnt a huge amount, often in creative and exciting ways, in the company of other women exploring these new (at the time) ideas. I particularly wish to name Women in Theology and the St Hilda Community as two communities where my own theological thinking was pushed forward in creative and innovative ways. Many friends and colleagues have also shared in the shaping of my ideas over the years: too many to mention all by name. At the risk of offending some whom I shall omit from this list, I am particularly grateful for conversations and explorations with

Mukti Barton, Helen Cameron, Gavin D'Costa, Daphne Hampson, Peter Kettle, Brenda Lealman, Kate Lees, Mary John Marshall osb, Rosie Miles, Janet Morley, Anne Peart, Anne Pounds, Alan Race, Ruth Shelton, Sue Tompkins, Hannah Ward and Jennifer Wild. I am also grateful to my editors at DLT for their patience and encouragement in the production of this text.

1. INTRODUCTION TO FEMINIST THEOLOGY: CONTEXT AND KEY CONCEPTS

The emergence of feminist theology

Feminist theology, or more properly, *theologies*, has emerged in modern times as a challenge to the male bias in religion and society as a whole. Although feminist theology has many significant roots in pre-modern history, in women's struggles for justice within the church, and in women's religious experiences and writings from the earliest centuries, it has only emerged as a fully conscious movement with its own literature, spokespersons, principles and methods in the past few decades. Influenced and empowered by the secular women's movement of the late 1950s and early 1960s, as well as by the Civil Rights movement in the United States and liberation theology from Latin America, the first critical feminist theological work emerged from the States at the beginning of the sixties and from there spread to Europe and the rest of the globe. The work of pioneering figures like Mary Daly, Letty Russell, Rosemary Radford Ruether and Elisabeth Schüssler Fiorenza, all working in North America, was followed by the emergence of traditions of feminist theology in every continent on the globe. Nevertheless, we should not assume that the foundations of feminist theology are exclusively white and western for, as Kwok Pui-Lan points out, 'the emergence of white feminist theology in the contemporary period was not an isolated phenomenon, but was embedded in the larger political, cultural, and social configurations of its time' (2002, p. 26). At any rate, within a very short period of a few decades, feminist theology has become a global movement situated in many settings, and drawing on many different political, philosophical and religious roots to express, in a multitude of voices, its concerns and convictions. Every area of theology – systematic or dogmatic theology, biblical studies, church history, pastoral theology, ethics and so on – now has substantial contributions from diverse feminist perspectives which multiply almost daily.

Feminist theology, like liberation theology, should not be seen primarily or exclusively as an academic phenomenon. It has strong roots in a grass-roots movement of women and men trying to live out a more inclusive and liberating Christian faith in which women have full visibility and equality of access and can articulate their faith experience in ways that are valued by all. Communities, groups and networks of women (and some men too), both within and beyond the churches, provide the primary context where people meet together to worship using forms they have developed themselves, to read and reflect on the Bible and other texts in the light of their own struggles and needs, to share their experiences of God and try to find new language and metaphor to name such experience, and to act together to challenge sexism and other forms of oppression in church and society. One of the dangers as feminist theology becomes more established in the universities is that it is losing touch with this grass-roots foundation and becoming alienated from the urgent needs and concerns of those whose passion and energy should fuel it. First and foremost, it is a social movement for justice and wholeness of life in God, not only at the personal level, but also at the interpersonal, the political and, indeed, the cosmic level, for feminists have much to say about our relationship to the earth and how patriarchal theologies have profoundly damaged the earth. All the philosophical sophistication which is now evident within feminist theological debate must serve that larger end of liberation.

Reflecting on experience

How far has feminism influenced your life? Think about your upbringing, your education, your work environment, and so on.

How far has feminism impacted on church life in your locality, if at all? In what ways?

What different attitudes towards feminism are present in your family and close circle?

What would you say your own attitude towards feminism is?

What are you hoping to learn or achieve from studying feminist theology?

Key concepts and principles of feminist theology

There is no one feminism and no single feminist theology. Feminist theologians come from many different faith traditions, cultures, backgrounds and academic persuasions. In this study, we are mostly considering *Christian* feminist theology, but even within these limits there is still enormous variety. Nevertheless, there are certain fundamental principles, or what Susan Frank Parsons (2002, pp. 114ff.) calls 'dogmas' of feminist theology – broad, underlying convictions which most, if not all, feminists hold, and which underpin and shape the enterprise of feminist theology in its many different guises. All of these are the focus of much critical debate in contemporary feminist theology, but it is essential to have some grasp of them if you are to understand what feminism and feminist theology is about.

The structural injustice of sexism

According to feminism, human community is characterised by a basic structural injustice, a distorted relationality between the sexes, such that men as a group have power over women as a group. This basic inequality has characterised all known history, is universal and is enshrined in language, culture, social relations, mythology and religion. The most fundamental feature of this distorted relationality is a pervasive **dualism** which makes a sharp distinction between perceived male and female roles, psychic qualities, characteristics and areas of responsibility, valuing those identified with the male as inherently superior to those identified with the female. For example, masculinity is identified with rationality, power and initiative, whereas femininity is identified with emotion and intuition, weakness and passivity – and these are not equally valued. This dualism is established socially, in the social relations assigned to men and women – men dominate in the public sphere, women in the private, for example – but is ratified at the level of mythology, ritual and theology. The patriarchal God upholds and is at the apex of this dualistic system. God is associated with the male and identified with masculine characteristics such as those already mentioned, and is cast over and against the female.

Such an analysis of sexism sees the relation between the sexes essentially in structural or systemic, not individual, terms. Clearly, individual males vary enormously in their attitudes to and behaviour towards women; not all men are misogynist. Nevertheless, this does not change the fact that human society is structured in such a way as to advantage men and disadvantage women. Men *as a group* have power over women collectively. Although both men and women suffer from sexism, and humanity as a whole is distorted, they do not suffer equally. The structural inequality functions systematically to disadvantage and disempower women.

A key consequence of sexism is **androcentrism** – the bias of society and culture towards the male, the assumption that the male is norm. Androcentrism functions at every level of human culture and society: in its history, traditions, language, arts, professions, and so on, all of which have been controlled and monopolised by men. A consequence of androcentrism is that women are systematically excluded and obliterated from historical traditions and contemporary thought-forms, and thus rendered invisible to themselves and others. Think of the way in which, traditionally, the arts have been conceptualised and practised, for instance. It is frequently claimed that there are few great women artists or musicians, but this reflects the ways in which visual art and music have been conceptualised and organised, as much as the actual contributions which women have made to these fields. Women have made music and visual art down the ages at least as much as men, but much of women's creative work has been collaborative, anonymous and passed down orally (in the case of music) or categorised as 'craft' (for example, women's needlecraft) rather than 'art', and therefore of inferior status.

Sexism and androcentrism are the twin major features of **patriarchy**, a much-used concept in feminism, which refers to the entire system of oppression, injustice and exploitation that operates between the sexes. Patriarchy (literally, the power of the fathers) refers to the social system in which sexism operates, a social system which is organised entirely on the basis of male domination of women. Elisabeth Schüssler Fiorenza (1995, p. 14) has suggested that it is more accurate to think in terms of what she calls *kyriarchy*, the rule of the emperor/master/lord/father/husband over his subordinates, since this is able to encapsulate other forms of oppression such as racial, class and economic, as well as gender oppression. Most feminists recognise that there are multiple forms of interlocking oppressions, of which sexism is only one, and that it is necessary to address all forms of oppression if all women are to be liberated.

The grounding of theology in women's experience

All theology is done on the basis of experience, whether this is acknowledged or not. Most theology in the past has been done almost exclusively from the perspective of male experience; men have been those who have written, taught and preached about the meaning of faith, and women have been excluded from such offices and opportunities that would have allowed them to study the faith. Nevertheless, theology has been 'gender-blind': it did not recognise the partiality and bias of its pronouncements, but offered them as universally valid and applicable to all humanity, women as well as men. As Ursula King puts it, 'One must . . . ask how the creation and formulations of one sex alone can possibly be universally valid for all people, women and men?' (King, 1989, p. 163). Now women are doing their own theology, and 'have become the subject of a new theological approach rather than simply being the object of theology' (*ibid.*). By insisting on doing theology from the perspective of women's experience, feminists are both calling attention to the androcentrism of previous theology and seeking to redress the imbalance of a religious tradition in which the dominant forms of thought and expression have been owned and controlled by men.

Women's experience is called upon as both *source* and *norm* in feminist theory. It is the substance, material and evidence upon which theology is developed and built, on the one hand; and it is the norm against which all theories and claims are judged, on the other. Thus, women use their experiences of oppression, relationships, sexuality, motherhood and so on, as a major *source* for reflecting on reality, and test all theological claims and doctrines against the *norm* of that experience. In a much-quoted passage, Rosemary Radford Ruether expresses this principle as follows:

> The critical principle of feminist theology is the promotion of the full humanity of women . . . Theologically speaking, whatever diminishes or denies the full humanity of women must be presumed not to reflect the divine or an authentic relation to the divine, or to reflect the authentic nature of things, or to be the message or work of an authentic redeemer or a community of redemption. (Ruether, 1983, pp. 18–19)

A good deal of discussion has centred on the notion of 'women's experience' in recent feminist writing (e.g. Hogan, 1995). As Susan Frank Parsons (2002, p. 117) suggests, 'beginning with experience is not . . . without its philosophical or theological problems . . . For whom does a woman speak?' It cannot be assumed that women the world over share anything in common beyond the fact of their exclusion and misrepresentation, but even here, some women have been more profoundly alienated and oppressed than others, especially poor women and black women, but also lesbian and bisexual women, women with physical or mental disabilities, old women and working-class women. The notion of a global, undifferentiated women's experience has been discredited in favour of a much more nuanced and critically aware understanding of different women's *experiences*, which includes attention to differences of race, class, culture and social location.

Listening and looking for difference
The need to extend the notion of 'women's experience' beyond simplistic assumptions of a common, undifferentiated unity of all women everywhere leads to the formulation of this principle. This has become a prominent commitment within recent feminist theory, rooted in the assumption that no matter how much like another human being one person may be, there is always difference present and there is always potential for these differences to be different over time. These differences exist between and among women, and thus, as Sandra Harding puts it, 'There will be many different feminist versions of "reality", for there are many different realities in which women live, but they should all be regarded as producing more complete, less distorting, and less perverse understandings than can a science in alliance with ruling-class masculine activity' (1986, p. 157). What this means for feminist theology is well expressed by Linda Hogan:

> A theology based on women's experience and praxis must of necessity acknowledge and learn to value difference . . . A theology based on an understanding of women's experience and praxis, which is sensitive to racial, class and sexual differences among women, must recognise women's 'different primary emergencies'. (Hogan, 1995, p. 167)

In other words, feminist theology must beware of making any generalised statements about the meaning of God, the church or Bible for women, since any one woman will be speaking from one particular situation and vantage point, and cannot speak on behalf of all women. What this means in practice is at least two things: first, each woman in writing or speaking must be open and explicit about her own context and the limitations of her perspective, and second, feminists must be committed to dialogue and exploration with other women in different situations and with different experiences, so that they can broaden and enrich their own limited perspectives.

Commitment to liberating and empowering women

This is sometimes known as the 'advocacy' or 'standpoint' position, or the 'praxis' or 'empowerment' principle. There is an insistence that theology arises directly out of life experience and must flow back into experience. Theology must not be isolated in the ivory tower of academia but must take root in the streets and the homes of ordinary women and men, and must be orientated to the transformation of society; and particularly to the liberation and empowerment of women. Theology which has, in the past, fuelled and legitimised women's oppression must now become a tool and resource for women's empowerment. What makes theology feminist according to this principle is not merely the subject-matter or content (i.e. theology *about* women) or the gender of the theologian (i.e. theology *by* women) but the commitment to doing theology with the specific goal of empowering and liberating women (i.e. theology *for* women).

This advocacy standpoint of feminist theology carries on the tradition established by liberation theology of theology taking up a clear stance on the side of the oppressed and in opposition to the oppressor. Liberation theology insists that no theology can be politically or socially neutral; if it claims to be, it is merely masking its own political stance (usually on the side of maintaining the status quo). Liberation theologians have familiarised us with such notions as God's bias towards the poor. Feminist theologians apply this basic principle of advocacy to the sexual oppression of women and take up a deliberate stance on the side of the freedom and liberation of women. In such an approach, God does not take up a bias towards the poor or towards women because they are any better (or worse) than the rich or men, but precisely because they are oppressed.

Exercise

Think of some examples from both society and church of ways in which sexism, dualism, androcentrism and patriarchy have functioned.   ▶▶

What do you think it means for theology to be done from the perspective of women's experience? What difference might this make,
for example, to reading the Bible, interpreting the nature of God
and Christ, or understanding the church?

What are the dangers of universalising women's experience? What
key differences between women need to be kept in mind?

Do you agree that theology can never be neutral? What political,
theological and practical commitments do you think should be at
the heart of Christian theology?

Different traditions within feminist theology

As stated above, there is no single feminist theology but many different
types and forms of feminist *theologies*. As we proceed, I shall attempt to
demonstrate something of the range of feminist perspectives on the
different theological subjects we will be looking at. However, it may be
helpful at this stage to map out at least some of the major dividing lines
between feminist theologians of different schools, persuasions and from
different contexts. Broadly speaking, it is possible to suggest a number
of divisions, clustered around certain key issues about which feminists
are divided, although it should be recognised that any classification is
partial and can never capture the whole picture. Accepting this, we can
say that, first, feminist theologians are divided on their analysis of
religious systems and the solution to their corruption; second, they are
divided on their analysis of the human condition and the remedy for its
unjust state; third, they operate from a range of diverse social and
cultural contexts and these shape their differing emphases and concerns
profoundly.

First, then, feminists are agreed that religion has been profoundly
shaped and distorted by sexism, but they disagree when it comes to the
possibility of reform. **Christian feminists**, such as Elaine Storkey (UK),
Letty Russell (US), Mercy Amba Oduyoye (Ghana) and Aruna
Gnanadason (India), to name but a few, affirm that Christianity is still
capable of being reformed so that it may become truly inclusive of all
humanity – although not without huge and wholesale change. (There
is a wide divergence between Christian feminists in terms of how

much change is deemed to be necessary and possible whilst still maintaining a distinctive Christian identity, with more conservative feminists holding on to more of the tradition, and radicals arguing for more far-reaching transformation.) On the other hand, **post-Christian or post-traditional feminists,** such as Mary Daly (US), Daphne Hampson (UK) and Carol Christ (US), argue that it is a hopeless case: Christianity – and other patriarchal religious traditions – are irredeemably sexist and the only solution is to leave and forge a new religious consciousness which is based on women's experience. **Feminist thealogians** (*thealogy* from the greek 'thea' or goddess, and 'logos', study or reflection upon) such as Christ, Starhawk (US), Melissa Raphael (UK) and Beverley Clack (UK), are those who embrace the notion of a female symbolic world-view and orient their thinking and praxis around the figure of the Goddess.

Second, feminists are agreed that there is a fundamental injustice in the relationship between the sexes, but they analyse that relationship differently and recommend different solutions to the injustice. **Liberal feminists,** coming out of the Enlightenment tradition shaped by values of equality, fraternity and rationality, affirm the basic equality of all human beings who share a common human nature characterised by reason and moral conscience. All are entitled to common, equal rights, without distinction. Thus the project of liberal feminism is to extend by social reform the rights enjoyed by men in the free world – citizenship, suffrage, ownership, education, and so on – to women. This is the common popular notion of what feminism is about, and many feminist theologians have been widely influenced by the liberal tradition, though few nowadays would identify wholly with it. **Romantic feminists** affirm male and female as complementary opposites which, together, constitute human being and reflect the image of God. However, in this view, the male has become corrupt through the exercise of power, and it is the female who represents salvation and wholeness. Thus the project of romantic feminism is to recover and celebrate the lost feminine principle, however this is defined, and structure social reality anew according to feminine values. There is a tendency to reverse the traditional patriarchal order and stress the female as representative of ideal humanity, which the male has lost and must reclaim. Romantic feminists include separatists like Daly who argue for the redemption of humanity through women, as well as much more conservative biblical feminists who argue for the distinctiveness and the complementarity of the sexes in God's design. **Radical or Marxist feminists,** such as

Rosemary Radford Ruether (US), Carter Heyward (US) and many womanist theologians, affirm humanity as male and female and as potentially revelatory of the image of God, but assert that, because male and female exist in a structurally unjust relation, both masculinity and femininity as traditionally defined represent different types of human alienation from its full potential. Neither role extension nor role reversal will achieve a redeemed humanity; only a radical restructuring of social reality will release women and men to become a new humanity. Thus radical or revolutionary structural change is the project of radical feminism.

Whilst liberal and romantic feminism tend to operate with essentialist views of humanity – that is, believing that there is an enduring core or central 'essence' which constitutes human being (in the case of liberalism identified as the generic human being, in the case of romanticism identified as contrasting essential female and male types) – radical feminism has a more dynamic and historically relativist understanding of human nature, seeing human nature as historically changed and changing. **Post-modern feminists** reject any notion of a permanent, unchanging self or a particular 'essence' of human being around which feminists can unite; rather, they posit a much more fragmentary, differentiated notion of human being which celebrates diversity and the freedom to create the self anew continuously. Many contemporary feminist theologians are strongly influenced by, and seek to engage with, postmodern perspectives, particularly as they are represented by the French linguistic 'schools' of Luce Irigaray and Julia Kristeva, even if they do not wholly align themselves with their philosophical commitments. Grace Jantzen, a feminist philosopher of religion, and Susan Frank Parsons, an ethicist and dogmatician, are examples of British feminists currently engaging seriously with postmodern views.

Whilst the above differences cluster around theological and philosophical issues about the nature of religion and the nature of human personhood, another dividing line within feminism is across the diverse social, cultural and political contexts within which feminists operate. Although feminists worldwide share a common struggle against injustice, the injustices and struggles faced by women in Asia or Africa are not the same as those faced by women in Europe or North America. Black and Asian women struggle against the 'double oppression' of sexism and racism in a way which marks out their experience from that of white women. Women in different cultural contexts face very different social and religious challenges, whether this be issues of female circumcision in Africa, the status of the dalits in India or women's experiences of 'han' (unrequited suffering) in Korea, as well as broader, shared issues of colonisation, enculturation and poverty caused, at least in part, by western domination and exploitation. This has led to a rich variety of different types of feminist theology from different parts of the world and different cultural contexts. **Womanist theology** has been claimed as a distinctive form of black feminist theology, represented by African Americans such as Delores Williams, Jacquelyn Grant and Katie Cannon, as well as southern-hemisphere feminists such as Mercy Amba Oduyoye (Ghana), Virginia Fabella (Philippines) and Elsa Tamez (Latin America). Spanish-speaking women in the States have developed their own forms of Hispanic, Latino or **Mujerista** theology, whilst Asian feminist theology has its own distinctive forms of expression, drawing on Korean **Minjung** theology of the exploited masses (Chung Hyun Khung speaks of women as the 'minjung of the minjung') and Indian **dalit** theology of the so-called 'untouchables', as well as other liberation struggles, such as efforts to counter female feticide and dowry deaths. Ursula King (1994, pp. 16ff.) suggests that 'third-world' feminist theology is marked in particular by a strong emphasis on praxis, on the commitment to life, justice and freedom from oppression; a sharing of the depths of oppression, suffering and struggle against the realities of poverty, racism as well as sexism; a strong note of hope in the face of apparent despair; a strong experience of church-as-community; and a more concrete notion of liberation than is often found in first-world feminist theologies.

Other kinds of difference between feminist theologians could be noted: different theological and academic paradigms shape the ways in which feminist theologians approach the doing of theology, whether as biblical hermeneutics, systematic theology, philosophy of religion or intercultural discourse (see Parsons, 2002); and it makes a big difference whether feminists are working primarily within an academic milieu or at a grass-roots level. At this stage, I do not attempt to discriminate between all these different differences, but simply alert readers to the immense wealth of variety and riches currently present within the field.

EXERCISE

This exercise is intended to help you encounter and explore something of the diversity of feminist theology as it exists around the globe today. Using EITHER the worldwide web OR the indexes of some reference works listed below, make a search of two or three of the following, making notes about each as you go.

- Feminist theology
- Feminist spirituality
- Women and religion
- Womanist theology
- Mujerista theology
- African feminist theology
- Asian feminist theology
- Ecofeminist theology
- Christian feminism
- Post-Christian or post-traditional feminism
- Goddess movements
- Wicca
- Thealogy
- Women and religion
- Womenchurch (or Women-church)

Further reading

Fiorenza, E Schüssler (1996), *The Power of Naming: a concilium reader in feminist liberation theology*, New York/London, Orbis/SCM, Part 1.

Isherwood, L and McEwan, D (1993), An introduction to feminist theology and the case for its study in an academic setting, *Feminist Theology*, 2, 10–25.

Isherwood, L and McEwan, D (1993), *Introducing Feminist Theology*, Sheffield, Sheffield Academic Press.

Parsons, S F (ed.) (2002), *The Cambridge Companion to Feminist Theology*, Cambridge, Cambridge University Press, chapters 1 and 2.

Storkey, E and Hebblethwaite, M (1999), *Conversations on Christian Feminism: speaking heart to heart*, London, Fount/HarperCollins.

Reference works

Isherwood, L and McEwan, D (eds) (1996), *An A to Z of Feminist Theology*, Sheffield, Sheffield Academic Press.

King, U (ed.) (1994), *Feminist Theology from the Third World: a reader*, London, SPCK.

Loades, A (ed.) (1990), *Feminist Theology: a reader*, London, SPCK.

Russell, L M and Clarkson, J Shannon (eds)(1996), *Dictionary of Feminist Theologies*, London, Mowbray.

2. TEXTS OF TERROR OR EMANCIPATORY DISCOURSE? THE BIBLE IN FEMINIST PERSPECTIVE

Introduction

The Bible is regarded as the authoritative and normative witness to divine revelation in Christian tradition. It provides Christianity with its dominant narratives, images and symbols, and is a primary source in preaching, teaching, prayer, worship, doctrine and ethics. But the Bible is also a deeply patriarchal and androcentric text. This causes problems, not only for women readers, but especially for them. This chapter demonstrates some of these problems by examining the invisibility of women in scripture, the inferiority of women in scripture and the sexism of the processes of transmission and interpretation in the post-biblical era. We wrestle with the question, how can women read an ancient patriarchal text as a liberating and empowering word of God? Various strategies for re-reading the scriptures developed by feminists are then described, which, taken together, can offer creative ways forward. A variety of understandings of the Bible emerge from this discussion, all of which challenge any naïve or simplistic identification of the Bible with the word of God.

Reflecting on experience
Reflect on your own experience of reading and hearing the Bible.
- What difference does it make that you are a male or a female reader?
- How does this influence and shape *what* you hear, *how* you hear it and what *meaning* and *value* it has for you?

Reading the Bible as women

Women have been reading the Bible for centuries, but they have not necessarily been conscious of reading the text *as* women. With the rise of the modern feminist movement in the late nineteenth century, some women began to assert the importance of reading the biblical texts self-consciously as women, bringing their own life-experience and perspective to bear on the texts. Writing in 1889, Frances Willard, president of the Women's Christian Temperance Union, declared, 'We need women commentators to bring out the women's side of the book; we need the stereoscopic view of truth in general, which can only be had when woman's eye and man's eye together shall discern the perspective of the Bible's full-orbed revelation' (Willard, 1889, p. 21). *The Woman's Bible*, a remarkable collection of commentaries on the Bible by a group of radical American women in 1895, was perhaps the first systematic attempt to bring the 'woman's eye' to the text – and not only scandalised many devout believers of the time but also split the American feminist movement in two. Although Elizabeth Cady Stanton and her team of commentators were not scholars (they could not be, since women at that time had no access to formal theological study), they brought a lively and spirited critique to the texts. They read the Bible with a 'hermeneutics of suspicion', challenging rather than accepting the 'man's eye' view, and exposing the sexism of the texts, pointing out, for example, how Eve was blamed for the Fall and how women's roles in many stories were marginal.

Today, we are heirs to a century and more of women's writings on the Bible, coming out of every context in which the Bible is read – from many different cultures, from churches and convents, classrooms and meeting places, city streets and base communities, political campaigning groups and women's refuges – all the varied places where women gather to share their lives and to seek inspiration or encouragement from the Bible. This immense library of feminist biblical hermeneutics is hugely varied, and does not speak with one voice. Scholars have developed many different, often very sophisticated, methods for reading the scriptures, whilst those working outside academia have brought different pressing concerns to their readings of the texts. We cannot hope to engage with all these perspectives in one short chapter, but we can note some of the key questions and issues which have been raised by women in these different settings.

The problem of the Bible for feminists

What do women notice when they begin to read the Bible self-consciously as women? We notice many things and we do not notice the same things. Nevertheless, women readers over the last century have consistently noticed a number of aspects that are problematic, which make the reading of the Bible as the revealed word of God difficult, if not impossible.

The invisibility of women in scripture

In page after page, women are simply *absent* from the biblical texts. It has been estimated that only about one-tenth of the Bible is explicitly about women or women's lives. The majority of biblical characters are men. The Old Testament centres on the history of patriarchs, judges, kings and prophets, all of whom were men. Only two books in the Bible are named after women – Ruth and Esther. Women are very largely incidental to the text, brought into the narratives in terms of their relation to men as wives, mothers and daughters, rather than in their own right. For example, what we know about Sarah and Hagar is restricted to their roles as child-bearers of Abraham's offspring, and Miriam's role in the leadership of Israel is largely incidental to the text, which concentrates on Moses and Aaron. Where women are the focus of interest, they are often regarded as exceptional rather than as representative of their sex. So, for example, Deborah was renowned as a female judge precisely because she was an exceptional case; the wisdom and beauty of the Queen of Sheba were proverbial – but how many other female monarchs are named in scripture? The laws address adult males, not women. In the Decalogue, the last commandment stipulates, 'You shall not covet your neighbour's house; your neighbour's *wife*, or his man-servant' and so on. It is clear that both the one being addressed and the 'neighbour' to whom the text refers are male. The female is excluded from the text, not only in the sense that the text is not *about* her but also, and perhaps more significantly, in the sense that the text is not *addressed* to her: the assumed reader is male.

Women fare rather better in the New Testament, particularly in the gospels, where there are many incidents that centre on Jesus' meetings with women, conversations with them and relationships with them. Nevertheless, the New Testament is by no means unproblematic for women. Jesus' teaching, for example, seems to assume a predominantly male audience. Only four out of his entire body of parables feature women as central characters. The world of the parables is a man's world, populated by kings, merchants, builders, farmers, masters and slaves, fathers and sons (Slee, 1990). In Paul's letters, in the Acts of the Apostles, in other epistles, women's lives are far from visible. By and large it remains the case that the male is the norm.

The inferiority of women in scripture

Even where women do appear in the texts, it is clear that their status, position and value are largely assumed to be lesser than that of men. This reflects the patriarchal world-view of the biblical era, in which women were generally regarded as inferior to men, as infantile or incomplete persons. Phyllis Trible summarises the situation thus:

> Less desirable in the eyes of her parents than a male child, a girl stayed close to her mother, but her father controlled her life until he relinquished her to another man for marriage. If either of these male authorities permitted her to be mistreated, even abused, she had to submit without recourse . . . The narrative literature makes clear that from birth to death the Hebrew woman belonged to men.
>
> What such narratives show, the legal corpus amplifies. Defined as the property of men (Exodus 20:17; Deuteronomy 5:21), women did not control their own bodies. A man expected to marry a virgin, though his own virginity need not be intact. A wife guilty of earlier fornication violated the honour and power of both her father and husband. Death by stoning was the penalty (Deuteronomy 22:13–21). Moreover, a woman had no right to divorce (Deuteronomy 24:1–4) and most often, no right to property. Excluded from the priesthood, she was considered far more unclean than the male (Leviticus 15). Even her monetary value was less (Leviticus 27:1–7).
>
> (Trible, 1990, p. 24)

This estimation of women is, indeed, questioned within other parts of the scriptural tradition, particularly in the New Testament. Jesus challenges certain aspects of the legal situation, as is evident in his treatment of the woman caught in adultery (John 8) and his teaching on marriage and divorce (Mark 10:2ff.; Matthew 19:3ff.; Matthew 5:27ff.). He treated women with dignity and respect in a manner certainly unusual, if not exceptional, for his day. Yet Daphne Hampson (1990, p. 88) claims that 'there is no positive evidence that Jesus saw anything wrong with the sexism of his day'. Certainly in the post-resurrection situation of the church, there is much evidence of conformity to the prevailing patterns of male-female relations in the Roman household (e.g. 1 Corinthians 11:2ff.; 14:33ff.; Ephesians 5:21ff.; Colossians 3:18ff.; 1 Timothy 2:11ff.), which subordinated the female to the male. It is difficult to claim a total equality of the sexes in the New Testament tradition as a whole.

From a historical perspective, none of this may be surprising. The biblical texts emerge out of an ancient patriarchal culture and reflect patriarchal values and norms. But what does this mean for women believers reading the text today? How can women situate themselves in relation to texts that appear to assume or even demand their invisibility and subservience?

The sexism of the processes of transmission and interpretation

The biblical texts themselves, then, are clearly problematic for women. But it is not only the texts *per se* which are problematic; it is also the ways in which the texts have been used, interpreted and handed on to subsequent generations which constitute another layer of the problem. The texts have come down to us through thousands of years of translation and interpretation, a complex process almost wholly in male hands. We read the texts today 'through' this long tunnel and this profoundly shapes how we hear and receive them.

This complex process of transmission and interpretation has functioned in a number of different ways to render the biblical texts oppressive for women. In many cases, texts and traditions about women have been ignored and sidelined in preaching, teaching, commentary and exegesis. Thus, we have heard little about Hagar's meeting with God in the wilderness, or the role of the midwives Shiprah and Puah in the Moses story, or about Miriam's leadership of her people. In the New Testament, few sermons have been preached about Martha's confession of faith, whilst Peter's has been applauded for centuries; the woman who anointed Jesus for burial in Mark's Gospel has disappeared into obscurity, whilst Judas is a name recognised across the world as a byword for betrayal. Sometimes translations even 'wrote out' women from the text, such as feminine name endings being changed to masculine ones in New Testament epistles, where the writer greets Christians by name.

More perverse and problematic than simple sidelining of texts about women has been the tendency of scriptural exegesis to distort the biblical traditions in order to uphold stereotypical views of women, which, themselves, have been used to legitimise women's subordination. Eve has been presented as the temptress and seductress, responsible for sin in a way not true of Adam, justifying male headship and supremacy; Mary the mother of Jesus has become the plaster-cast image of sexless compliance, reinforcing women's passive obedience, not only to God but also to men; Mary Magdalene, the apostle of the apostles, has been perverted into the sexual sinner, sister of Eve, and all women have been regarded as potential temptresses; Martha becomes the fusspot in the kitchen rather than the woman of great faith and insight represented in John 11, and woman's domestic labour has thereby been trivialised at the same time as her ability to engage with theological ideas repressed. Then there has been the overt, polemical and political use of the scriptures by those in authority to underpin and justify women's subordination: texts such as Genesis 3, and Paul's injunctions to the Corinthian women to keep silent (1 Corinthians 14:33ff.) have been shorn from their context and universalised to endorse women's submission in church and home.

EXERCISE

'The [biblical] text is the product of a sexist, indeed misogynist, culture: the presuppositions are written into it. Moreover, such texts are the more dangerous in that they affect us at a subconscious level' (Hampson, 1990, p. 92).

How would you respond to this challenge, and some of the problems outlined above?

Feminist readings of scripture

How can women continue to read the Bible as 'holy scripture', the 'word of the Lord', when it is so thoroughly sexist? Many different strategies have been developed by feminist biblical scholars as ways of reading the texts 'against the grain' of their original patriarchal context and intention. These strategies do not change the nature of the texts as such, but they may provide creative ways of engaging with the texts so that their liberatory potential is released. We consider three such strategies below.

The recovery of neglected texts

The first approach concentrates on recovering lost or neglected traditions within the Bible which positively celebrate women's lives. Thus, feminists have recovered a strong, if marginal, tradition of female God-language in the Bible in which metaphors of giving birth, mothering and nursing are applied to God. Others have worked to recover women's stories in the history and traditions of Israel and the church, pointing out the significant roles that women played, for example, in the Exodus narratives or the crucifixion and resurrection stories. Others again have worked to recover women's stories from 'between the lines' of scripture, by detailed 'detective work' on the texts where women are mentioned perhaps only by name or in passing. Such work has been engaged, not only by biblical scholars such as Elisabeth Schüssler Fiorenza, Phyllis Trible and others, but also by artists, poets and story-tellers. Lucy D'Souza's marvellous 'hunger-cloth' of biblical women brings alive neglected biblical stories using conventions of Indian iconography, whilst British novelists and poets such as Sara Maitland, Michele Roberts and Carol Ann Duffy 'read between the lines' to reconjure neglected biblical women such as Mrs Noah, Hagar and Sarah, Mrs Lazarus and Pilate's wife, using imagination to recreate what historical memory has lost.

This is very important compensatory work, making up for the centuries of interpretation in which women's history has been almost wholly ignored. More than that, it cleverly subverts and challenges the 'man's eye' view of things, casting the whole text into a different light. Yet the approach on its own has its limitations. It ignores the vast majority of the biblical texts in which women are absent, and so it does not answer the pressing question of how women are to read *those* texts. By concentrating on the recovery of past traditions, it may ignore the great gulf that exists between women's lives in biblical times and women's lives today. How does it help me as a modern woman to identify with a biblical woman living in the past? This is an important hermeneutical issue.

EXERCISE

Choose a biblical text in which a woman or women feature significantly or incidentally. Write the story from the perspective of the woman character. This approach can also work in texts where you 'invent' or 'insert' a woman into the text. For example, try writing the story of Luke 15:11–32 from the perspective of the (absent) mother, or the prostitute. Depict the wedding at Cana (John 2:1–11) from Mary's viewpoint, or create the Syro-Phoenician woman's account of her meeting with Jesus (Mark 7:24–30).

The intention of this exercise is to engage creatively with the texts, not to recreate what 'really happened'.

Reading texts 'in memoriam'

The second approach is also concerned with reading texts which have to do with women, and concentrates on the employment today of the memories of biblical women to inspire resistance to patriarchy and the promotion of women's liberation. Phyllis Trible has developed this approach in her book *Texts of Terror*, as a way of reading damaging biblical traditions about women. In this exegesis of four Old Testament narratives of the abuse, rape, murder and dismemberment of women (Genesis 19, Judges 11: 29–40, 2 Samuel 13 and Judges 19), Trible does not play down the horrific nature of these texts; if anything she highlights it. We cannot read these texts as holy scripture in the sense that we cannot share their evaluation of women or their ethical perspective. Indeed, we must protest against the values which they portray. But we may read these texts 'in memory of' the biblical women whose sorry stories they tell, mourning their suffering and making a determined commitment to end such treatment of women in our own time. Thus Trible sees her work as that of interpreting stories of outrage 'on behalf of their female victims in order to recover a neglected history, to remember a past that the present embodies, and to pray that these terrors shall not come to pass again' (1984, pp. 2–3).

More broadly, much of Fiorenza's biblical recovery work, focused on the retrieval of the lives of women in the early Christian communities, has been inspired by a similar concern to honour and draw on the memories of biblical women. Fiorenza suggests that the stories of such women may be a spiritual heritage for women today. We cannot *copy* their lives, but we can emulate their faithfulness in the very different conditions of our own time.

We participate in the same struggle as our biblical foresisters against the oppression of patriarchy and for survival and freedom from it. We share the same liberating visions and commitments as our biblical foremothers. We are not called to 'empathize' or 'identify' with *their* struggles and hopes but to continue *our* struggle in solidarity with them. Their memory and remembrance . . . encourage us in historical solidarity with them to commit ourselves to the continuing struggle against patriarchy in society and church. (Fiorenza, 1984, p. 115)

This second approach is a helpful addition to the first, for it acknowledges more explicitly the gulf that exists between the biblical world and our own, and wrestles with 'hard texts' without obscuring the reality that some of the biblical material about women is deeply hurtful for women today. Rather than excising such material from the collective consciousness of the church, it proposes that we 'remember them', in much the same way as contemporary Jews insist that the Holocaust must be remembered, precisely so that its ghastly history is not repeated.

EXERCISE
📖 **Read one of the so-called 'texts of terror'.**

- What is your reaction to the story?
- What does it mean to read the story 'in memory of' women?
- How would you read such a text publicly in a church service? Could you say, at the end of it, 'This is the word of the Lord', as is common in some churches?
- If you had to preach on the text, what would you say?

The 'golden thread' approach

A third approach attempts to find a way of reading the whole biblical text, not simply those texts which are about women. It acknowledges the great variety and diversity of the biblical literature, and takes fully seriously the patriarchal world-view of the biblical writers. It is a method which attempts to bring some order to the many diverse – sometimes contradictory – things which the scriptures can be said to be about, and to make sense of the frankly 'hard texts' of the Bible. In this approach, an underlying principle or key is identified as the central focus of scripture, permeating all its many disparate strands. This principle or key is then used to interpret other passages of scripture, even where the principle itself may not be in evidence, as well as to interpret contemporary situations not foreshadowed in the Bible itself.

The method of the golden thread approach itself is an ancient one, going back at least as far as Luther. What is new in feminist approaches is the choice of the golden thread. The best example of this approach in feminist biblical exegesis is Rosemary Radford Ruether's working of liberation as the key with which to unlock the meaning of scripture. Ruether sees the principle of liberation as the key prophetic-liberative principle of the Bible, testified to throughout the biblical writings, but particularly in the prophetic tradition, the Exodus narrative and the Kingdom praxis of Jesus. Whilst this principle is infrequently applied specifically to women in the Bible itself (though it is occasionally, for example in the prophetic concern for the plight of the widow and Jesus' liberating concern for women), nevertheless it is legitimate to extend the principle now to women in contemporary culture, as well as to use the principle to criticise those parts of scripture which do not live up to the vision of liberation. The Bible itself may not be consistent in applying the principle of liberation to women's situation, but *we* can – and must.

Another example of this kind of approach is my own work on the New Testament parables (Slee, 1990), in which I identify the disrupting, destabilising impact of the kingdom as the thread running through all of the parables. Whilst the parables themselves rarely apply this notion of the subverting power of the kingdom to women's lives (except occasionally, such as in Luke's parable of the widow and the judge), we may legitimately do so and claim biblical authority for doing so. This third approach is important insofar as it provides a way of reading the whole of scripture meaningfully. It is perhaps the most flexible methodology, for it allows great divergence between the biblical texts themselves and the modern situations to which the texts may be applied, whilst still claiming some continuity. Its dangers are twofold: first, the choice of the golden thread may be arbitrary and reflect the limitations of the exegete rather than the biblical witness itself; second, the exegete may attempt to manipulate scripture to 'fit' one interpretative key and thus deny the richness and variety of the biblical literature.

EXERCISE

Consider what guiding principles you have used, either consciously or unconsciously, in your reading of the Bible to help make sense of its diversity.

- From where have these guiding principles or interpretative keys come?
- Have they changed over time?

The radical challenge of feminist exegesis

Whichever approach is taken to reading scripture, feminist exegesis challenges at its root the understanding of the Bible as the revealed, inspired word of God, at least as this has often been understood. For how can the Bible be the word of God if it commands and legitimates female suppression? Is it not shown to be merely the fallible words of men? As Fiorenza puts it, 'if we proclaim that oppressive patriarchal texts are the Word of God then we proclaim God as a God of oppression and dehumanization' (1984, p. xiii). Many feminists feel they have no choice but to frankly set aside the Bible as a damaging patriarchal text which can only reinforce women's oppression. Others do not reject the Bible wholesale, but wish to supplement it by other texts in which women's subjectivity is centre-stage. Ruether, for example, has come to the conclusion that the Bible on its own is insufficient as a text for women seeking liberation from patriarchy. The Bible can still be helpful for women if read with one of the above methodologies, but, in addition, alternative texts are needed which speak more clearly about women's lives and experiences.

Similarly, Fiorenza proposes that the Bible cannot be read as a 'timeless archetype' whose word is binding for all time, as Christians in the past have attempted to do, and as many continue to do. Rather, the texts must be read as a 'historical prototype open to its own critical transformation' (1984, p. xvii). Instead of reading scripture as 'mythical archetype' which 'takes historically limited experiences and texts and posits them as universals, which then become authoritative and normative for all times and cultures', we are invited to read scripture as 'historical prototype' which 'places biblical texts under the authority of feminist experience [and] maintains that revelation is ongoing' (1984, pp. 10, 14). Women today should read the Bible as a record of the struggles of Jews and Christians to be faithful to their understanding of God in their own times and situations. We stand in line with their struggles, and may read their struggles as a heritage to encourage and empower us, but we are not to copy their behaviour or beliefs as such, since the beliefs and actions required of faithful believers in our own time will be very different. Read in this way, revelation is located not in androcentric texts themselves, but in 'the experience of God's grace and presence among women struggling for liberation from patriarchal oppression and dehumanization' (1984, p. xvii).

EXERCISE

How far do the ideas in this chapter challenge or change your understanding of the Bible?

- In what sense, if at all, can women read the Bible as 'word of God'?
- What other texts might you want to place alongside the Bible to supplement, critique and expand its own witness?
- Does this relativise or enhance its authoritative status?

Further reading

Cullen, M (1998), *The Word According to Eve: women and the Bible in ancient times and in our own*, London, Penguin.

Newsome, C A and Ringe, S H (eds) (1992), *The Women's Bible Commentary*, London, SPCK.

Ruether, R R (1985), *Womanguides: readings toward a feminist theology*, Boston, Beacon.

Russell, L M (ed.) (1985), *Feminist Interpretation of the Bible*, Oxford, Blackwell.

Selvidge, M J (1996), *Notorious Voices: feminist biblical interpretation 1500–1920*, London, SCM.

Stanton, E C (1985, abridged edition), *The Woman's Bible*, Edinburgh, Polygon.

Trible, P (1984), *Texts of Terror: literary-feminist readings of biblical narratives*, Philadelphia, Fortress.

3. WHAT LANGUAGE SHALL I BORROW? RELIGIOUS LANGUAGE AND MODELS OF GOD

Introduction

The way in which we speak of God is of fundamental importance, for our language about God both reflects and shapes our most fundamental convictions about the nature of truth, our human and cosmic destiny, and our own human nature, since we affirm we are made 'in the image of God'. Right speech about God, Elizabeth Johnson suggests, 'is a question of unsurpassed importance' (1992, p. 3), *the* central question of any theology, for 'the symbol of God functions as the primary symbol of [a] whole religious system, the ultimate point of reference for understanding experience, life, and the world. Hence the way in which a faith community shapes language about God implicitly represents what it takes to be the highest good, the profoundest truth, the most appealing beauty' (p. 4). But language about God does not only *reflect* our deepest convictions; it also *shapes* thought and experience. The way in which we speak about God has a profound, if mysterious, impact upon our understanding of and attitudes towards our own humanity and that of our neighbours, and shapes behaviour in powerful and subtle ways. The symbol of God functions to undergird and legitimate a whole system of myth, story and theology, a whole way of thinking, a whole way of life.

Reflecting on experience
What image of God do you hold? Where has this image or notion come from? What are its sources and influences?

Has your thinking about God changed much over your life? How and why? ▶▶

Consider the following names and images of God and reflect on which ones you are familiar with, which ones you use in speaking about or to God, and which ones are strange or new to you: King, Lord, Judge, Shepherd, Rock, Light, Lover, Spouse, Brother, Mother, Child, Eagle, Bread, Water, Love.

Try drawing or painting your image of God, or write about the names of God.

A critique of patriarchal God-language

Although it is formally proclaimed and doubtless sincerely believed by the majority of believers that God is spirit and beyond gender, the overwhelming majority of terms and images used to speak of God in Christian tradition have been, and remain, drawn from male experience. God is named and known as Father, Lord, King, Judge, Shepherd, (male) Lover, Master, Ruler, and so on. In classical theism, female images were rarely or never employed. Whilst historically the doctrine of the Trinity was developed to subvert hierarchical understandings of the Godhead and, arguably, exists to protect *against* an overliteralised, androcentric model of God, the dominance of Father/Son imagery in trinitarian thought has, in fact, reinforced hierarchy and the maleness of God. Thus the message is given that 'God is male, or at least more like a man than a woman, or at least more fittingly addressed as male than as female' (Johnson, 1992, p. 5).

The use of male images for God is not problematic in and of itself. What is problematic, as Johnson suggests, is that male images are, or have been, used exclusively, literally and patriarchally. First, male imagery is used **exclusively**. Until very recently, male images have been used to the exclusion of female or other, for example, animal, images of God, even though both of these are present in scripture. Such exclusive use seeks to repress and deny the presence of female God-language in Christian tradition and thus render it impossible to break out of male hegemony. Such language is in danger of becoming irrelevant, Sallie McFague (1983) suggests, because it no longer speaks to the reality of people's experience but is perceived as excluding whole realms of the experience of women, black people and other marginalised groups. Secondly, male imagery is used **literally**. Although officially denied, where God-language is exclusively masculine, it comes to function in a literal sense, at least subconsciously. We no longer recognise the metaphorical nature of the language we are using about God, but identify it literally and unequivocally with the symbol. The gap between symbol and reality is closed. We come to think that God really *is* male. This is dangerous because we cease to be critically aware of the limitations of our God-language and are in danger of idolising particular, limited, metaphors of models of the divine. Thirdly, male imagery for God has been used **patriarchally**. Not only are male images used to speak of God, but also they are particular *kinds* of male images, which cluster together into one dominant, patriarchal model of ruling male power. The dominant model of God in classical Christian tradition is that of the ruling male monarch (invariably white) who has absolute control over his realm and subjects and who demands obedience and obeisance. This is reflected in pictorial imagery of God as the old bearded man seated on a throne, but also more subtly in classical theology in which the transcendence, omnipotence, omniscience and impassability of divinity are stressed. Although Christianity contains within itself the seeds of radical subversion of this model of the patriarchal God, especially in the preaching and praxis of Jesus, and in the very notion of the incarnation, even Christology itself soon came to model and mirror this picture of God: Christ became elevated into a ruling king seated alongside his Father whose maleness and power merely reinforce the patriarchal model.

Feminists argue that the effects of such patriarchal God-language are profound. 'The symbol of God functions', as Johnson puts it (1992, p. 5). The symbol purveys profound messages both about the nature of divinity and of humanity, about where divine power and authority are vested in the world, about the ways in which God acts and manifests. We can distinguish between a number of levels upon which the symbol operates and shapes attitudes and behaviour. When God is spoken of only in male terms, this has profound **psychological effects** upon women's sense of identity and psychological well-being. The implicit message to women is that masculinity is somehow more god-like, nearer to godliness, preferred in some way over against femininity, and that to be female is not to be capable of imaging the divine nature. As Mary Daly famously put it, 'If God is male, then the male is God' (1986, p. 19). A survey by Jean Aldrege Clanton (1991) suggests that the exclusive use of masculine God images contributes to women's feelings of unworthiness. Women who thought and spoke of God as masculine scored more highly on an abasement scale than those who held androgynous or gender-transcendent images of God. At the same time, Clanton suggests, 'exclusive masculine images of God damage men as well as women. Whereas women find reinforcement for passivity in these masculine images, men find support for pride and control. They are tempted to think more highly of themselves than they ought and thus to control more than they should' (p. 81).

Religious symbols function not only at the personal level, but also at the social. They legitimate certain ways of relating between persons, certain ways of holding power, certain ways of structuring society. According to feminists, 'patriarchal God symbolism functions to legitimate and reinforce patriarchal social structures in family, society, and church. Language about the father in heaven who rules over the world justifies and even necessitates an order whereby the male religious leader rules over his flock, the civic ruler has domination over his subjects, the husband exercises headship over his wife' (Johnson, 1992, p. 36). This kind of argument is used quite overtly by those who argue that women cannot be ordained as priest, for example, or those who hold to the notion of male headship within the family. We can see, then, that the male image of God has profound **sociological effects**.

The exclusive use of male God-language also functions **theologically**. It idolises certain understandings of God and limits the scope of divine self-disclosure. 'Divine mystery is cramped into a fixed, petrified image' (Johnson, 1992, p. 39). This is what McFague names as *idolatry*, where we come to identify our language for God with Godself, and, ironically, it is one of the most basic sins castigated within the scriptures. Thus, it is not only oppressive to women to name God only as male, 'it is idolatrous to make males more "like God" than females. It is blasphemous to use the image and name of the Holy to justify patriarchal domination' (Ruether, 1983, p. 23).

EXERCISE

Make a critical study of the God-language in a selected act of worship: either in your own church (if you attend one) or in a church you don't know; or video a broadcast service such as 'Songs of Praise'. If possible, have some of the key texts, such as hymns or prayers, in writing so that you can study them closely.

▶▶

- What were the dominant images of God used? Where were they from? (Scripture? Tradition? Contemporary sources, such as films or books or art? Personal experience?)
- How were these images used? Were they offered authoritatively? Were they challenged or questioned in any way?
- Analyse the psychological, sociological and theological effects of the God-language used. Would certain groups of people have been able to relate to these images more than others? What implicit messages were conveyed by the language used?

Feminist strategies for speaking of God

If exclusive patriarchal God-language is damaging to both women and men psychologically and sociologically, and limits what we can know of the mystery and wonder of God, how then can we speak of divine presence in more adequate ways? A number of different responses to this question can be identified in the work of contemporary feminist theologians, some more radical and far-reaching than others.

Feminine 'traits' or 'characteristics' in God

The first response we might name as a minimal one, which seeks to make the least change to existing ways of speaking about God. This approach seeks to give 'feminine' qualities to God, who is nevertheless still imagined predominantly as a male person. This approach is represented by a number of theologians; for example, Moltmann (1981) speaks of the 'motherly Father' God of Jesus, and Congar (1983) speaks of the maternal, tender traits of God. This way of including the feminine may have some positive effects in introducing gentle, nurturing elements into the patriarchal model of God and in countering the worst excesses of sexism; but it is unsatisfactory for a number of reasons. It does little to challenge the fundamental androcentrism of patriarchal God-language – the male still remains the norm, but is enlarged slightly to include the feminine. It also leaves unchallenged the basic dualist and stereotypical notions of 'masculinity' and 'femininity' which feminists want to challenge: the female is still associated with qualities such as gentleness, nurturing, and so on, whilst the male is still associated with power, strength and control. It does not substantially change hierarchical gender relations.

A feminine 'dimension' in God

A second, more radical approach is to uncover and model a feminine 'dimension' in God, usually the Holy Spirit identified as the female dimension of the Trinity, but sometimes Mary championed as a female archetype, or even Jesus feminised as the maternal dimension within the Godhead. This approach has some grounding in scripture and tradition, where the Spirit is spoken of in female images and is associated particularly with the creative, nurturing power of God to bring forth life in creation, in the spiritual life of the individual, and within the community of the church. Such an approach is represented in recent Catholic theology by Boff (1987) and Gelpi (1984), and by feminist theologians such as Alwyn Marriage (1989), in her book *Life-Giving Spirit*. It does have more far-reaching effects than the first approach, in taking seriously the capacity of the female to name God, and in relativising the hegemony of the male. But it still preserves the ascendancy of male power; putting it crudely, two out of three persons of the Trinity remain male. And, since in Christian tradition the Spirit has often been subordinated to the Father and the Son, the problem of female subordination is perpetuated. As with the first approach, this one tends also to fall into the trap of essentialising and stereotyping male and female characteristics rather than challenging them.

Female and male as equivalent models of God

This third approach is distinguished from the two above in that it posits 'speech about God in which the fullness of female humanity as well as of male humanity and cosmic reality may serve as divine symbol, in equivalent ways' (Johnson, 1992, p. 47). This approach shares in common with the first two approaches a preference for human, personal metaphors and models of God, but it insists that both maleness and femaleness in their full humanity can image and symbolise God, and that both are necessary for pointing towards the full mystery of God, since no one image or symbol can ever capture or contain the fullness of that mystery. This approach also seeks to move beyond stereotypical or essentialist notions of maleness and femaleness. It recognises that what it means to be male and female is not timeless, fixed or universal, but is dynamic, shifting and culturally conditioned.

This approach takes a number of different forms, and can be found in both ancient and modern versions. Mystics such as Anselm and Julian of Norwich famously named God and Jesus in terms of motherhood, but also drew on many other gendered images to name God as lover, father, husband and friend. Many contemporary feminist theologians intermingle female-specific, male gendered and non-gendered models for God, such as Mother, Lover and Friend (McFague, 1987), Spirit-Sophia, Jesus-Sophia and Mother-Sophia (Johnson, 1992), or Mother, Woman and Shaman (Kyung, 1991). Janet Martin Soskice (2002, p. 144) talks about 'the play of gendered imagery' when both male and female images are used with 'rhetorical excess', such as we find in the ancient Syriac *Odes of Solomon* in which not only the Spirit is feminised, but also the Father as well:

> A cup of milk was offered to me
> And I drank it with the sweetness of the Lord's kindness.
> The Son is the cup,
> And He who was milked is the Father,
> And she who milked Him is the Holy Spirit.
>
> (in Soskice, 2002, p. 144)

Where many images are juxtaposed in tension and developed in extreme forms, they have the power both to provoke novel insight and experience of God *and* to reinforce the limitation and fancifulness of all human speech about God.

The recovery of the Goddess

Moving beyond a position of accepting male and female images as equivalent ways of speaking of God, other feminists take a different way, emphasising the need for female God-language and imaging divinity in exclusively female terms as Goddess. For such thealogians, patriarchal models of God are so damaging that they are beyond repair, the patriarchal forms of speaking of God so dominant in classical monotheism that only a wholesale embrace of the feminine can compensate for this imbalance. Thealogians such as Carol Christ, Naomi Goldenberg, Starhawk, Melissa Raphael and Asphodel Long are committed to recovering ancient prehistoric traditions of the Goddess as well as to creating new models and forms of Goddess practice and worship. The Goddess movement is wide-ranging and includes a number of different strands: it overlaps, to some extent, with neo-paganism, witchcraft and Wicca, but, in contrast to them, has a specifically feminist commitment and concern in reclaiming Goddess imagery for the liberation and well-being of women. It is primarily a spiritual, rather than an academic movement, with strong ritual elements which 'celebrate the human connection to the cycles of the moon and the seasons of the sun, invoking the mysteries of birth, death, and renewal, joy and gratitude for finite life' (Christ, 2002, p. 81). It is plural and loosely formed, with no one authoritative text or tradition; it is anti-dualistic and anti-patriarchal, with a strong emphasis on nature and the earth, and holds an ethics of interdependence of all things in the web of life. Despite its many different forms and manifestations, the Goddess symbol is regarded as crucial for women:

> The importance of the Goddess symbol for women cannot be over-stressed. The image of the Goddess inspires women to see ourselves as divine, our bodies as sacred, the changing phases of our lives as holy, our aggression as healthy, our anger as purifying, and our power to nurture and create, but also to limit and destroy when necessary, as the very force that sustains all life. Through the Goddess, we can discover our strength, enlighten our minds, own our bodies, and celebrate our emotions. (Starhawk, 1989, p. 24)

Whilst at first sight a long way from orthodox Christian belief and practice, the Goddess movement represents an important challenge to and critique of the church, for it affirms the 'underside' of Christian orthodoxy: those aspects of human experience (such as the body, the senses, sexuality, femaleness *per se*) and cosmic reality (the earth, the seasons and cycles of growth and decay) which have been neglected and even demonised by an overly cerebral, word-based and male-based religion. Whilst some critics suggest it reinscribes those very dualisms it seeks to overcome in its romantic and essentialised view of femaleness, it is a significant and creative movement in our time that has proved life-giving for many women who have not found nourishment in traditional institutional religion.

Non-gendered or personalised speech about God

A different reaction to the limitations of masculine imagery for God is to give up gendered language altogether and seek for broader human terms which encompass both male and female without differ-entiation. God becomes Parent rather than Father or Mother, Lover or Partner rather than Husband, Child rather than Son. God the Trinity is named as Creator, Redeemer and Sustainer, rather than Father, Son and Holy Spirit. Such language can have its uses in pointing away from gender and sexuality as the locus for naming and knowing God; but that is its very weakness, for it may convey a somewhat abstract, generalised knowledge of God which is far from the incarnational focus of Christianity. The power of a metaphor is precisely in its concreteness and particularity, and language which smooths out the shock of the particular may lose much of its power. More interesting are attempts to speak of God which go beyond the human, personalised realm completely, such as Mary Daly's proposal of God as Verb, Rosemary Radford Ruether's notion of 'God/ess' as a new way of referring to the divine and Carter Heyward's relational speech about God.

In *Beyond God the Father*, Daly jettisons patriarchal God-language in favour of a way of speaking about transcendence as the 'Verb of Verbs', which is actualised through the commitment to the self-realisation of women:

> Why indeed must 'God' be a noun? Why not a verb – the most active and dynamic of all? Hasn't the naming of 'God' as a noun been an act of murdering that dynamic Verb? And isn't the Verb infinitely more personal than a mere static noun? The anthropomorphic symbols for God may be intended to convey personality, but they fail to convey that God is Be-ing. Women now who are experiencing the shock of nonbeing and the surge of self-affirmation against this are inclined to perceive transcendence as the Verb in which we participate – live, move, and have our being. (Daly, 1986, pp. 33–34)

Ruether speaks similarly of divinity who is known in and through the self's struggle to come into authentic being. We encounter God/ess when we are liberated from the false and alienated world and come into touch with our authentic selves, in and through healed relationships with our bodies, with other people, and with nature. Her proposal for naming this reality is more of a literary than an auditory one, since it cannot be *said* in such a way as to bring out its gender-ambiguity. 'We have no adequate name for the true God/ess, the "I am who I shall become". Intimations of Her/His name will appear as we emerge from false naming of God/ess modelled on patriarchal alienation' (1983, p. 71).

Carter Heyward, like Ruether, emphasises that God is known in and through relationships to self, other and world, but more unequivocally than Ruether, defines God in strongly relational terms as 'the power of relation'. In opposition to traditional notions of transcendence, Heyward speaks of a God who is intimately related to the world, who is source of all relational power and active justice-seeking and who calls for the voluntary participation of human beings in making right relation on the earth here and now:

> Without our touching, there is no God.
> Without our relation there is no God.
> Without our crying, our raging, our yearning, there is no God.
> For in the beginning is the relation, and in the relation is the power that creates the world through us, and with us, and by us, you and I, you and we, and none of us alone.

(Heyward, 1982, p. 172)

In practice, not all of these different responses to the renewal of God-language are mutually exclusive. Thus, a number of theologians wish both to speak about God in personalised, female terms such as Mother or Goddess, *and* to use gender-inclusive personalised terms such as Friend and Lover, *and* to employ non-human models and metaphors of God. As Brian Wren (1989, p. 143) suggests in his hymns, we need to 'bring many names, beautiful and good' to point towards the mystery of the 'Name Unnamed, hidden and shown, knowing and known'.

This does not mean that any and every image is to be accepted without critique. Important questions remain to be asked about how images are used, from where they are drawn, and what relation they bear to each other. Issues of authority and normative status remain; why should we use some images rather than others? How far are scriptural images normative? Or the images offered us by Jesus? If they are not, what norms are we to employ? Whatever images we employ, there will probably be controlling ones which organise the others. How should we decide what the controlling images are? In Christian tradition there are strong arguments for the dominance of personal symbols, not least the doctrine of the incarnation which hallows human experience as a major source for knowledge of the divine. But the Christian doctrine of creation also hallows the wider natural world as a source of knowledge of God, so non-human images and symbols need not be ruled out (indeed, they are legion in scripture).

These are complex questions which are not easily or quickly resolved. We seem to be in a time of major upheaval and transition, when old models are being critiqued and jettisoned, but there is no consensus about new ones to replace them. It is a time of experimentation. There is risk in such fluidity and experimentation, but without the risk and playfulness of current experimentation with models of God perhaps we shall not be able to discern the Spirit's work of new self-revelation in our time. This does not mean we are not called to serious work: the work of praying into our images of God, old and new, with attentiveness and care; the work of theological scrutiny of our images, paying particular attention to their psychological, sociological and theological effects; the work of relating insights from scripture, tradition, contemporary experience and reason in new and more satisfactory understandings of God for our time. This work is not only to be engaged by professional theologians, but by all people of faith as we seek to renew the language we have inherited from past generations of Christians.

EXERCISE

EITHER Make a critical study of some hymns and prayers written by contemporary writers such as Brian Wren, Jim Cotter, John Bell, Janet Morley and Jan Berry.

- What new images of God are present in their work? How are they used and developed?
- What is their impact upon you? What fresh insights or challenges do they open up?

OR Try writing your own prayer or poem addressed to God using one, two or more of the following images. If possible, share this exercise in a group setting, so that you can compare a range of different responses.

- Mother
- Lover
- Jester
- Friend
- Midwife
- Bakerwoman
- Traveller

- Child
- Baby
- Animal
- Rock
- Darkness
- Abyss
- Dance

Further reading

Daly, M (1985), *Beyond God the Father: toward a philosophy of women's liberation*, London, Women's Press.

Grey, M (2001), *Introducing Feminist Images of God*, Sheffield, Sheffield Academic Press.

Johnson, E (1992), *She Who Is: the mystery of god in feminist theological discourse*, New York, Crossroad.

McFague, S (1983), *Metaphorical Theology: models of God in religious language,* London, SCM.

McFague, S (1987), *Models of God: theology for an ecological, nuclear age,* London, SCM.

Parsons, S F (ed.) (2002) *The Cambridge Companion to Feminist Theology,* Cambridge, Cambridge University Press, chapters 5 and 8.

Ruether, R R (1983), *Sexism and God-Talk,* London, SCM.

Wren, B (1989), *What Language Shall I Borrow?* London, SCM.

Liturgical texts

Morley, J (1992), *All Desires Known,* London, SPCK.

St Hilda Community (1997), *Women Included: a book of services and prayers,* London, SPCK.

Ward, H, Wild, J and Morley, J (eds) (1995), *Celebrating Women,* London, SPCK.

4. DEADLY INNOCENCE? SIN IN FEMINIST PERSPECTIVE

Introduction

'All have sinned and fall short of the glory of God', St Paul declares (Romans 3:23). From early in Christian tradition, the doctrine of 'original sin' was propounded as an explanation both of the fallen condition into which all persons are born and of the effects that follow from sinful human nature. Augustine gave the classic account, based on a reading of the Genesis myth of the Fall, which has continued to shape western thought. He taught that in the pre-lapsarian state, human beings were subject to God, and the body subject to the soul, but that this rightful ordering of human nature was overturned by the sin of the Fall – understood essentially as the sin of pride, in which Adam and Eve turned away from dependence on God. As a result, human nature became corrupt, and intellect, will and body profoundly disordered. The lust and guilt resulting from this are transmitted afresh to each generation.

Whilst in principle Christianity proclaimed the universality of sin, there is a long and powerful tradition which has associated sin in particular with women, perceiving woman as the primary sinner, inherently more morally frail and liable to temptation than man, and, in some sense, responsible for bringing sin into the world and perpetuating its results. This tradition has two historical roots: the Jewish myth of the Fall, in which Eve ate of the forbidden fruit before offering it to Adam and was thus held to be more culpable than the man; and a second strand of Hellenistic thought which taught, on the basis of false biology, the idea of women as misbegotten male. Out of these twin roots, Christianity developed a distinctive understanding of woman as the 'weaker sex', which has had catastrophic effects on women's self-image, well-being and treatment by men down the ages.

> ### Reflecting on experience
> What does the notion of sin mean to you? From where have you derived your understandings?
>
> What does the notion of sin mean in popular culture? What images of sin can you identify in popular adverts, songs, films, and so on?
>
> Think of ways in which women have been portrayed in art, theology and popular culture as 'the weaker sex'. How far do you think this is changing?

Everywoman an Eve

Let us consider in a little more detail the ways in which the myth of the Fall has been read by theologians down the centuries as a statement of woman's responsibility for human sin. Whether the story itself suggests this interpretation is debatable (Mary Daly, for example, is in no doubt that the myth blames women, whereas Phyllis Trible argues that, if anything, women come out of the tale much better than men), and it is notable that Jewish tradition has had far less of a stress on woman's culpability, though it shares the same scriptures. This suggests that we are dealing here largely with *eisegesis* rather than exegesis, a reading *into* the scriptures of the prejudices and constructs of the surrounding culture rather than an authentic reading of the text. At any rate, the tradition of Eve as the 'type' of womankind is a long and tenacious one, in which Eve has been held to be guilty for setting in motion the series of encounters that end in the expulsion from paradise and the beginning of a state of existence characterised by pain, toil, alienation, and death. Church fathers and theologians down the ages read the story as a portrayal of women's moral frailty, sexual corruptness and guilt.

Eve/Woman as morally weak

This was a popular theme: the snake knew that Eve was morally weaker than her husband, therefore he tempted her first. Adam would not have succumbed if it had not been for Eve! Thus the poet Dracontius, writing at the end of the fifth century, asserts, 'The pitiless devil foresees that the man's brave heart may not be overcome by a serpent, so, under cover of a pious voice, he approaches the ears of his wife' (in Phillips, 1984, p. 57). A century or so earlier, Cyril of Jerusalem had written similarly, 'Not daring to accost the man because of his strength, he accosted as being weaker the woman' (Phillips, 1984, p. 57). Some centuries later, Martin Luther continues to perpetuate this tradition: 'Satan's cleverness is perceived also in this, that he attacks the weak part of human nature, Eve the woman, not Adam the man'. And again, 'Because Satan sees that Adam is more excellent, he does not dare to assail him; for he fears that his attempt may turn out to be useless. And I, too, believe that if he had attempted Adam first, the victory would have been Adam's. He would have crushed the serpent with his foot and would have said, "Shut up! The Lord's command was different!"' (in Miles, 1992, p. 109).

Eve/Woman as temptress/seductress

Eve ate the fruit and then gave some to her husband to eat. From this, it was deduced that Eve tempted or seduced Adam to sin. Woman, then, is seen not only as the morally weaker, but as the temptress, luring men into sin. It is, above all, in her *fleshliness* and sexuality that woman is the temptress; Eve is attractive and alluring to Adam, but precisely as such she is dangerous, for she causes the man to lose control of his reason and senses, and to fall into sin. (Note here the contradiction between this notion that the man could not resist Eve's attractions and the above theme of his moral superiority!) Thus woman's nature, her bodiliness and sexuality, are to be at the same time pre-eminently desired and dreaded. This theme, of the twofold desirability and fearfulness of female sexuality, is pervasive throughout western culture, and permitted Christian artists, poets and preachers to imagine and embody female nakedness and beauty whilst, at the same time, condemning them. The poet Dracontius demonstrates this kind of voyeuristic pleasuring in the female form:

> She stood before him, uncovered by any veil
> Her snowy body naked like a nymph of the sea,
> The hair of her head unshorn, her cheeks were made lovely with a
>   blush,
> And everything about her was beautiful: eyes, mouth, neck and
>   hands,
> Even as the fingers of the Thunderer could make her.
>
> (in Phillips, p. 33)

A medieval Armenian Gnostic tale tells how Eve's beauty was the cause of Adam's downfall: 'But when Adam saw the beauty of the woman, she robbed the reason from his head. At the same time that she was stripped of the [paradisiacal] garments of light, her body shone like a pearl' (in Phillips, 1984, p. 74). Thus it is that women's beauty is not to be trusted, is not what it seems, but is the cover for a licentiousness that will trap men and lead them into sin, and thinly veils women's shameful nature. The church fathers frequently betray this ambivalent and dualistic attitude to the female form; among them, John Chrysostom displays a particularly misogynist fear of the female body: 'Should you reflect about what is contained in beautiful eyes, in a straight nose, in a mouth, in cheeks, you will see that bodily beauty is only a whitewashed tomb, for inside it is full of filth.' For Chrysostom, as for many of the fathers, woman was a source of intractable paradox and confusion: 'What else is woman but a foe to friendship, an inescapable punishment, a necessary evil, a natural temptation, a desirable calamity, a domestic danger, a delectable detriment, an evil nature, painted with fair colours?' (in Phillips, 1984, p. 22).

Eve/Woman as scapegoat

Because it was Eve who first sinned, she comes to be held responsible for sin, guilty in a way not true of Adam, and thus to be punished by suffering and submission. Tertullian expounds the necessity of women's endless penitence and expiation in an oft-quoted passage:

> By every garb of penitence [Woman] might the more fully expiate that which she derives from Eve – the ignominy, I mean, of the first sin, and the odium [attaching to her as the cause] of human perdition . . . and do you not know that you are each an Eve? The sentence of God on this sex of yours lives in this age: the guilt of necessity must live too. You are the devil's gateway; you are the unsealer of that forbidden tree; you are the first deserter of the divine law; you are she who persuaded him whom the devil was not valiant enough to attack. You destroyed so easily God's image, man. On account of your desert – that is, death – even the Son of God had to die. (in Phillips, 1984, p. 76)

A medieval Irish poem puts the guilt in Eve's own mouth, thus alleviating men from the responsibility of scapegoating and punishing women:

I am Eve, the wife of noble Adam; it was I who violated Jesus in the past; it was I who robbed my children of heaven; it is I by right who should have been crucified.

I had heaven at my command; evil the bad choice that shamed me; evil the punishment for my crime that has aged me; alas, my hand is not pure.

It was I who plucked the apple; it went past the narrow of my gullet; as long as they live in daylight women will not cease from folly on account of that. There would be no ice in any place; there would be no bright windy winter; there would be no hell, there would be no grief, there would be no terror but for me.

(in Phillips, 1984, p. 77)

Such passages make for chilling reading, demonstrating as they do, all too clearly, the deeply entrenched misogyny of western Christendom. Ultimately, Daly argues, under the myth of the Fall, women become the victims to be punished, and finally destroyed, for their sin. The mass murder of thousands of witches in medieval Europe is not simply a historical aberration, but in a real sense, the horrific logical conclusion of the myth of female evil.

Eve/Woman as subject to Adam/Man

When women's sin is seen in these terms as the guilty act responsible for all evil in the world, what does it mean for women to be 'saved'? Primarily it means submission to male authority and control, both to the secular authority of the father or husband and to the religious authority of the church. Only by submission could women's defective moral frailty and dangerous seductiveness be tamed and controlled. The theme of woman's subordination was read out of the Genesis myth from two motifs in the story. First, because Eve was created second, out of Adam's rib, it was argued that she is 'naturally' subordinate to her origin and source. But secondly, woman is to be subordinate to man as a result of and a punishment for her sin, and, at the same time, as her own path to salvation. We find this kind of theology already taking root in the New Testament period, as is evident in the pastoral epistles:

Let a woman learn in silence with all submissiveness. I permit no woman to teach or to have authority over men; she is to keep silent. For Adam was formed first, then Eve; and Adam was not deceived, but the woman was deceived and became a transgressor. Yet woman will be saved through bearing children, if she continues in faith and love and holiness, with modesty. (1 Timothy 2:11–15)

The fathers developed what was embryonic in scripture. Thus, according to Augustine, 'even before her sin, woman had been made to be ruled by her husband and to be submissive and subject to him'; but, whereas this condition would have been maintained effortlessly and without resentment, after her fall, 'there is a condition similar to that of slavery', and the woman now deserves to have her husband for a master (Miles, 1992, p. 96). Much later, Luther similarly upholds this order; although he teaches that woman is necessary to man as companion, support and help, marriage is a mixed blessing in which punishment plays its part. Because of her sin,

> The rule remains with the husband, and the wife is compelled to obey him by God's command. He rules the home and the state, wages wars, and defends his possessions . . . The woman, on the other hand, is like a nail driven to the wall. She sits at home . . . [She] has been deprived of the ability of administering those affairs that are outside and that concern the state. She does not go beyond her most personal duties. (in Miles, 1992, p. 112)

The effects of 'false naming' on women

Mary Daly interprets the myth of the Fall as a 'prototypic case of false naming' (1986, p. 47); that is, it is a male myth which reflects the defective social arrangements between the sexes in a patriarchal culture, and, as such, it *mis*names the mystery of evil, as well as the reality of the relationships between men, women and God. Through this myth, women have become the scapegoats for human sin and the objects of male fear, hatred and punishment. Worse, women them- selves have internalised the myth and accepted its 'truth'. Daly sees four 'side effects' on women when this myth is accepted and internalised. First, there is psychological paralysis, a general feeling of hopelessness, guilt and anxiety over social disapproval; second, feminine anti- feminism is created – divisiveness among women themselves, and rejection of women by women; third, women display a false 'humility' – never aspiring 'too high', a strangely ambivalent fear of success, not being a rival to men; and fourth, women become emotionally depen- dent on men – unable to stand on their own feet, constantly needing male approval and affirmation. Women's real sin, then, according to Daly, is to have accepted and internalised the patriarchal lie, negated their own selfhood and abdicated responsibility for their own being and action in the world.

EXERCISE

Make a search of images of Eve in western art, architecture, poetry and theology. See if you can find images of Eve in churches in your locality. Visit a good art gallery, consult your local library, or do a search on the web. See if you can identify some of the themes above.

Feminist critiques of modern understandings of sin

At the same time as feminist historians were examining and deconstructing ancient readings of the Genesis myth, some feminist theologians were deconstructing contemporary male accounts of sin and suggesting that they exhibited an inbuilt androcentric bias – less blatant, less obvious, certainly, than the ancient teachings of the church fathers, but no less problematic for women. Valerie Saiving first pointed out the male bias in theological models of sin in an influential essay written in 1960. In this article, she analysed the theology of sin put forward by male theologians such as Paul Tillich and Reinhold Niebuhr, documenting their understanding of sin in terms of human pride, aggression, self-assertion, and will-to-power. Challenging the unquestioned notion of universal sin, Saiving argued that such a notion of sin corresponds far more closely to men's experience than to women's, for whom 'sin' is far more likely to involve such tendencies as 'triviality, distractibility, and diffuseness; lack of an organizing centre or focus; dependence on others for one's own self-definition; tolerance at the expense of standards of excellence; inability to respect the boundaries of privacy; sentimentality, gossipy sociability and mistrust of reason – in short, underdevelopment or negation of self'. In other words, whilst 'sin' for men may appropriately be thought of in terms of aggrandisement of the self, for women, it is much more likely to be negation of the self.

A number of feminists are unhappy with Saiving's account on the grounds that it reinforces gender stereotypes and rests on a kind of essentialism which is suspect on philosophical grounds, as well as ignoring cultural differences between women. It also perhaps remains rather preoccupied with *personal* sin and ignores wider social, systemic sin. It can even be seen as abdicating women from a proper responsibility for sin – Angela West (1995), for example, sees in much feminist theology an erroneous quest for a kind of ideological innocence and a projection on to men of the sins of the world, which simply reverses and perpetuates the scapegoating that women have experienced down the centuries. Whatever the limitations of Saiving's and similar approaches, her essay was enormously influential in beginning a debate about the nature and context of women's responsibility for sin, which has continued vigorously.

Alternative feminist theological models of sin

In traditional Christian theology, sin has been understood largely in terms of pride and aggression, the disobedience to God manifested by Adam and Eve. Because of the ambivalent attitude to the body and sexuality arising out of a dualistic patriarchy, the sins of the flesh have been emphasised perhaps above all others, and sexual sin particularly abhorred, whereas other sins, such as those of greed and the misuse of money, have been far less prominent. Feminist theologians have sought to develop alternative accounts of 'sin' and 'salvation' which arise out of women's distinctive experience and which speak to women's situation. We have already seen that Daly proposes that women's *real* or 'original' sin is to accept the patriarchal lie of woman as scapegoat, and to internalise the guilt. 'Salvation' thus begins when women reject the myth and false naming, and begin to affirm and name their own experience. We can identify several other feminist approaches to sin.

Sin as negation and neglect of the self

Saiving first propounded the notion that women's distinctive form of sin is likely to be an under-development of self in contrast to a typically male aggrandisement and over-extension of self. Later theologians, particularly Judith Plaskow (1980) and Susan Nelson Dunfee (1982), extended Saiving's analysis and discussion. The title of Dunfee's book, *The Sin of Hiding*, expresses well the notion that women have hidden from their own powers and gifts, have accepted the status of victim, and have been too ready to be passive and acquiescent. Far from being regarded as women's 'natural' state, by naming this as 'sin', feminist theologians protest in the strongest possible terms against women's own collusion with their oppression.

Sin as systemic structural injustice

As we have seen, some feminists have been unhappy with the narrowly personal focus of such accounts, and with their cultural limitations. Theologians such as Ruether, Williams and Thislethwaite focus, instead, on sin as systemic, social and political, rooted in the unjust relations of sexism, racism, classism and all discriminatory systems that are structured into the way societies behave and think. They have shifted the focus away from sin as solitary navel-gazing concerned with the rather petty weaknesses and inadequacies of individuals to a much broader notion which addresses the social and political realities of the nature of human community. Womanists such as Delores Williams played a prominent part in this development, calling attention to the 'double' and 'triple jeopardies' of racism, poverty and sexism under which women of colour suffer. Ecofeminists such as Ruether, McFague, and Deane-Drummond extend this analysis to the earth itself, calling attention to the ecological sins perpetrated against the earth by humanity, and argue that the dominance of nature by humanity is a key feature of the dualism that keeps power unequally distributed between women and men, black and white, poor and rich, animal and human. Such theologians call everyone to be accountable both for their personal actions and their actions as members of social, policial, economic and religious groups which perpetuate structures of injustice. Again, to name such injustices as 'sin' is both to assert their gravity and to call for their undoing; for sin is to be repented of, and this includes the systemic evils of which human beings are a part, as well as the personal sins of which we are aware.

Sin as the refusal of relation

A number of feminists offer notions of sin which helpfully draw together the personal and the political, rather than polarising them. For example, Carter Heyward proposes the notion of sin as 'the violation of right relation' (Heyward, 1989), McFague as the 'refusal of relationship' (McFague, 1993) and Ruether as 'distorted relationality' (Ruether, 1998, p. 71).

> Sin is our out-of-touchness with the fact that we are in relation – that our lives are connected at the root and that this is the sacred basis of our creatureliness, our humanity, our lives together on planet Earth . . . Weakened immeasurably by sin, generation upon generation, we do evil without having a clue that it is *evil* we are doing – the

countless ways we betray one another and ourselves: lying to those we love; turning our backs on the homeless; holding racism and other structures of injustice in place through fear, ignorance, or apathy; paying taxes that build bombs and missiles; floating through life in spiritual bubbles that seal us off from experiencing our shared Sacred Power to struggle against the systemic violence undergirding so much of our public policy as we enter a new millennium. (Heyward, 1999, pp. 84, 85)

Such a concept, which is a deeply biblical one, can illuminate personal as well as structural relationships. Because right relations are those which are mutually empowering, sin occurs whenever a person or group uses or abuses an individual, group or natural resource for their own purposes, thereby disempowering, degrading and all too often destroying who or what was used. As Ruether says, 'Sin as distorted relationship has three dimensions: there is a personal-interpersonal dimension, a social-historical dimension and an ideological-cultural dimension. It is imperative to give due recognition to all three dimensions, and not only to focus on the personal-interpersonal aspect, as our confessional and therapeutic traditions have generally done' (1998, p. 71). On the personal-interpersonal level, distorted relationship is evident wherever there is exploitation between individuals; but such patterns of domination are kept in place and reinforced by the structures of sexism, racism, classism and so on, into which we are born – the social-historical dimension of sin. These exploitative systems themselves are kept in place by 'ideologies that make themselves the hegemonic culture', that is, that 'make such unjust relationships appear good, natural, inevitable and even divinely mandated' (Ruether, 1998, p. 74). McFague (1993) focuses in particular on sin as refusal of relationship in the way we live in the cosmos; sin is our refusal to accept our rightful place in the scheme of things, to live as if we were not profoundly interconnected within the whole web of life, and this manifests in the form of living a lie in relation to other human beings, in relation to other animals and in relation to nature as a whole. Such understandings are not essentially out of tune with biblical notions, but apply them in fresh ways to contemporary contexts and issues.

EXERCISE

Matthew Fox suggests that Christianity, for the majority of its history, has been fixated with the notion of 'original sin' and has neglected the notion of 'original blessing'. This has led to a largely negative and pessimistic view of humanity, and has, ironically, resulted in human beings taking less than a full responsibility for their actions and the consequences of these actions in the world. How far do you agree?

Consider Heyward's model of sin as the refusal of right relation or in-touch-ness. How do you react to such a description of sin? What different examples of distorted or broken relationships can you think of? Remember to include relationships between different groups of people and wider structures as well as between individuals.

Have a go at writing your own definition of sin, in the light of the discussion in this chapter.

Further reading

Daly, M (1985), *Beyond God the Father: toward a philosophy of women's liberation*, London, Women's Press, chapter 2.

Grey, M (1989), *Redeeming the Dream: feminism, redemption and Christian tradition*, London, SPCK, chapters 1 and 2.

Hampson, D (1990), *Theology and Feminism*, Oxford, Blackwell, chapter 4.

Phillips, J A (1984), *Eve: the history of an idea*, San Francisco, Harper and Row.

Ruether, R R (1984), *Sexism and God-Talk*, London, SCM, chapter 4.

Saiving, V (1979), The human situation: a feminine view, in J Plaskow and C Christ (eds), *Womanspirit Rising: a feminist reader in religion*, San Francisco, pp. 25–42, Harper and Row.

West, A (1995), *Deadly Innocence: feminism and the mythology of sin*, London, Cassell.

5. CAN A MALE SAVIOUR SAVE WOMEN? CHRISTOLOGY IN FEMINIST PERSPECTIVE

Introduction

Classically, Christology has proclaimed Jesus as the Christ: that is, Jesus of Nazareth is proclaimed to be the one in whom the self-revelation of God is uniquely made known. This claim has been expressed historically in the doctrines of incarnation – that in Jesus God took flesh and became human – and Trinity – Christ as the Logos, the Second Person of the Trinity, co-equal and co-eternal with the Father and the Spirit. In modern times, there has been immense Christological ferment, as theologians and ordinary believers have attempted to reinterpret the meaning and significance of Jesus in contemporary cultural and philosophical terms, reflecting changing understandings of personhood, deity and historical particularity. In feminist theology too, the meaning and significance of Jesus Christ as the founder of Christianity and its primary symbol of God has been a central subject of debate. 'Precisely because it is the central symbol in Christianity, [Christ] is also the symbol most distorted by patriarchy', according to Ruether (1985a, p. 105), and thus most in need of reconstruction. Feminists have deconstructed traditional understandings of Jesus, as well as offered new, alternative versions of Christology in which the maleness of Jesus ceases to have significance or is radically reinterpreted.

Reflecting on experience

Is Christianity essentially a set of beliefs about Christ or a way of life inspired by Jesus? Or both?

▶▶

How far does it matter (to you, and to others) that Jesus was a man? Does this matter historically? Theologically? Psychologically?

What images of Jesus have shaped your thinking about Christianity? Consider visual images in books, paintings and church architecture, as well as 'mental' images you have received through teaching, popular perception and so on.

A feminist critique of Christology

All post-Enlightenment theology has had to grapple with the 'scandal of particularity' expressed in classical Christology, and it is not only feminists who have problems in accepting the classical doctrines. Since the Enlightenment, traditional Christology has increasingly come under attack, due to problems of the historical reliability of the gospel records, the difficulty in accepting the notion of uniqueness, the challenges of religious pluralism, and so on. But allied to such problems raised by modern consciousness, feminism poses particular challenges to Christology. The major problem for feminists is that, in the doctrine of Jesus as Christ, a male human being is identified uniquely with the person and activity of God. This gives rise to a number of interrelated problems.

The limitations of Jesus' attitudes towards, and teaching about, women

Because Christianity proclaims Jesus as the Christ, it looks to the teaching and practice of Jesus as peculiarly significant for revealing the ways of God. A number of feminists have challenged Jesus' behaviour towards women, concluding that, though it may have been forward-looking for its time, it is inadequate either as a basis for contemporary action or as grounds for proclaiming Jesus as the self-revelation of God. Daphne Hampson, for example, claims that, whilst Jesus may have had positive encounters with individual women, he did not see anything wrong with the sexism of his day or seriously challenge it.

> He suggests that a woman may be allowed to sit at his feet, rather than preoccupy herself with cooking. But there is no suggestion that the

service of others, in which discipleship was to consist, should involve taking some of the burden of housework from women. His parables never challenge male privilege. The father in the parable of the prodigal son divides his property between the sons. The owner of the house, the person who builds a house, and the one who has authority over servants, are all presumed male. In John 3 Jesus is reputed to have said that 'the bride exists only for the bridegroom'. Mention is made, in Matthew 18:25, of a man selling his wife and children into slavery to pay off his debt. What more need one say? (Hampson, 1990, p. 88)

Hampson argues that Jesus' message was addressed basically to men and consequently alienated women. Jesus' injunctions to give up land and possessions, not to initiate divorce, and to prioritise the demands of the kingdom over those of kith and kin, all appear to have been directed to men and to have been peculiarly difficult, if not impossible, for women to fulfil. 'The life which Jesus advocated must have necessarily had an appeal to men rather than to women, for it would in many cases have put women in an impossible position' (Hampson, 1990, pp. 88–89). Nor does Jesus challenge women's inferior position in the religious realm in any significant way, according to Hampson. She concludes, with Ochshorn (1981), that 'Jesus was neither a feminist nor a misogynist. His central message simply lay elsewhere' (1981, p. 173).

The symbolic significance of Jesus' maleness

A further and deeper problem for feminists resides in the pervasive male symbolism of Christology which, it is claimed, functions to legitimate sexism and androcentrism, and to exclude women from participating fully in the experience of redemption. Because Jesus was male, maleness comes to take on a symbolic significance over and above femaleness, such that it is claimed that only males can represent Christ at the altar or in the exercise of authority in the church. It may be *claimed* – and indeed was stated explicitly in patristic theology – that Jesus' *humanity* is what is significant for the work of redemption, *not* his maleness. (This underlies the patristic axiom, 'what is not assumed is not saved' – i.e. Jesus must 'assume' the human condition *per se*, not any specific manifestation of it, such as Jewishness or maleness, otherwise his redemptive work would be limited only to that section of humanity he represents.) Nevertheless, feminists claim that precisely because Jesus was a male human being, and that male human being has been proclaimed as uniquely revelatory of God, then the maleness of Jesus comes to take on a symbolic significance which belies the explicitly stated theological belief. Jesus as male saviour comes to ratify two of patriarchy's most powerful tenets, namely, the male as the norm (androcentrism) and the male as superior (sexism), because it is the male who was 'chosen' to embody the incarnation of God, and not the female.

Hampson points out that, in the past, the symbolic significance of Jesus as male was not so problematic, because it was generally accepted in western culture that men represented women also. This is now no longer the case, and the bias of male symbolism in Christianity 'may make God appear to be "male" in a way in which this was not earlier the case . . . A symbol which is a male symbol appears in our culture to represent maleness, in a way in which earlier this may not necessarily have been the case. Hence the urgency of the question as to whether Christ is an inclusive symbol, and the feeling of many women that it is not' (1990, p. 52).

The uniqueness and particularity of Jesus as the sole revelation of God

Allied to the above is a further problem. Feminism sharpens the dilemma raised by Christianity's claim that Jesus is the unique and sole revelation of God by asking, 'How can God's self-revelation be limited to one (male) individual in one period of remote, patriarchal history?' Ruether asks: 'Can Christology remain encapsulated in a single, "once-for-all" figure of the past who "completed" the work of salvation, even though we and our history remain obviously unredeemed?' (1985b, p. 112) The implicit answer here is evidently 'no'. Ruether suggests that we constantly need new images and understandings of the Christ-figure and of Christ's work, in order to appropriate the salvation of Christ. There is no one sacrosanct image or doctrine that can survive intact across centuries of historical and theological change. As modern and post-modern people, we have become increasingly sensitised to the realities of racism, sexism, and European chauvinism, and we can no longer 'read' or appropriate an exclusively male image of God as salvific. The image of Christ must take new forms, 'as woman, as Black and Brown woman, as impoverished and despised woman of those peoples who are the underside of Christian imperialism' (*ibid.*, p. 113).

The 'scandal of particularity' raises two particular problems for feminists. First there is what we might call a **theodicy problem** – that is, a problem concerning the morality of God's actions. If Christians claim that God chose to reveal him(sic)self uniquely in Jesus of Nazareth, feminists must ask why God chose the patriarchal conditions of that time for his self-disclosure, and why he chose to reveal himself through male human being, when such a choice would only reinforce and perpetuate the oppressive patterns of patriarchy. Hampson puts the issue forcibly: 'The question which feminism poses for Christianity . . . is whether Christianity is ethical. That is to say, is it not the case that a religion in which the Godhead is represented as male, or central to which is a male human being, necessarily acts as an ideology which is biased again half of humanity? Is it not the case that such a religion is by its very nature harmful to the cause of human equality?' And again, 'How can God be seen to be good when one considers what history has been, and what it has meant for women that God has been conceived in primarily male terms?' (1990, pp. 54, 11)

The second problem arising from the uniqueness of Christ is what we might call an **idolatry problem**. Feminists such as Mary Daly and Carter Heyward argue that Christianity encourages an unhealthy idolatry or Christolatry, an idolisation of Jesus as the one, unique revelation of God. This has many harmful consequences in human attitudes and behaviour, but is particularly harmful for women, because it reinforces women's tendency towards emotional dependence on men and it idealises the 'virtues' of sacrificial love, suffering, humility, meekness, and so on, which are often symptomatic of women's underdeveloped self. Instead of looking to find the God-image within themselves, and instead of taking responsibility for themselves and their own decisions, women are encouraged by Christology to look outside themselves to another – to a perfect, male Other – to provide guidance, authority, affirmation and self-worth. Thus, Heyward suggests that worship of Jesus as the Christ 'is a serious stumbling block for women because we must constantly look up – for inspiration, leadership, role-modelling, and redemption – to a man' (1984, p. 214). Daly argues that we must do away with the whole notion of looking to any one person or period as a role-model. 'What we are about is breaking models in the old sense of the term . . . Those who have come far enough in consciousness to break through the destructive conditioning imposed through "models" offered to the female in our culture are learning to be critical of all ready-made models' (1986, pp. 74–75).

EXERCISE

Consider the arguments above and how compelling they are.

- How far does it matter that Jesus was not a feminist in the modern sense? How would you describe his attitudes towards and relationships with women?
- How significant is the male, patriarchal imagery of traditional Christology? Can it be changed without doing violence to the historical particularity of Christ as a male first-century Jew?
- In what sense do you understand Jesus as a 'model' to be followed? How do you interpret the idea of Jesus' uniqueness? Does this set him apart from all other human beings, or might he be seen as a representative of all human beings?

Feminist Christologies

Feminist theologians have attempted to respond to these Christological problems in a number of ways. Reformist feminists have tried to restate Christological belief in such a way that it becomes consonant with feminism, and can take account of women's experience and needs. Post-Christian feminists such as Hampson and Daly have rejected Christology altogether, asserting that the belief in Jesus as Christ is no longer tenable for feminists. Here we will consider only the various reformist attempts.

Compensatory moves: Spirit or Mary as a complementary female principle

One way of responding to the male bias of Christology is not, strictly speaking, a move within Christology itself, so much as a compensatory move in some other area of Christian doctrine. Thus some more con-servative feminists such as Alwyn Marriage (1989) call on the Spirit as a counterbalancing female principle which compensates for the male symbolism of Jesus and the patriarchal Father God. Other writers seek to reinstate Mary as an 'icon' of divinity who can represent the feminine taken into divinity, as Christ represents maleness in divinity. Yet again, some religious groups, such as the Shakers, propose a female Messiah who stands alongside, and is equivalent in status and significance to, Christ. For the Shakers, the female Christ is the theological expression of the androgyny of God and God's image, humanity, which must be expressed in a redeemer from both the male and the female orders of humanity. The female as the last of God's works is the crowning glory of creation. So the appearance of the female Christ in Mother Ann Lee, the founder of the Shaker sect, is necessary to complete and perfect the redemptive revelation of God, who is both Father and Mother.

Naming Christ as Female: the Christa figure

Another possible response to the Christological dilemma is to reinterpret traditional symbols and formulas using female language and models. This is a way of taking absolutely seriously the Christian claim that Christ incorporates and represents the whole of humanity. Christ gathers up and represents male and female, young and old, rich and poor, black and white, and so on. If women are to believe this assertion, then they need to experience Christ imaged in a form they can recognise, i.e. in a female form. Thus a number of contemporary feminists write and speak of the 'Christa', the female Christ, and contemporary artists, such as Edwina Sandys and Almuth Lutkenhaus-Lackey* portray the crucified Christ in a female form. Interestingly, this is not an entirely modern phenomenon: there are depictions of a bearded, crucified female Christ-figure in medieval European devotional literature. Ruether provides justification for this move by calling attention to the way in which the Christian community continues Christ's identity and presence in the world today, and this community includes women, who may therefore represent Christ. 'In the language of early Christian prophetism, we can encounter Christ *in the form of our sister*. Christ, the liberated humanity, is not confined to a static perfection of one person two thousand years ago' (Ruether, 1983, p. 138).

Marcella Althaus-Reid has recently developed this notion of the female Christ in subversive and perhaps shocking terms in her *Indecent Theology* (1999, 2001). She images Christ not only as female but as a poor female, as prostitute, as leather-clad lesbian, dying next to her lover. Such images of Christ, like those of the 'disabled Christ' (Eisland, 1994) can shock and offend and, in doing so, raise profound questions about where we expect to find Christ present and at work. If not in real flesh and blood bodies in their manifold particularity, questings and yearnings for love and connection, then where?

---

* Examples of the female Christa can be found in *The Christ We Share* pack (USPG/CMS).

Reclaiming the historical Jesus: message Christologies

Another move, and a dominant one at that, in contemporary feminist Christology is to seek to retrieve a message-based Christology, rooted in the praxis and preaching of the historical Jesus and seeking to follow the *way* of Christ, rather than focusing on the worship of Jesus himself. This represents a 'low' Christological approach (in contrast to 'high' Christologies), so-called because it starts from the ground upwards, beginning with the humanity of Jesus and seeking to find in his humanity signs and intimations of divinity. Many modern, post-Enlightenment Christologies share this approach, in contrast to the dominant tradition throughout Christendom in which the humanity of Christ was obscured by his divinity. Rosemary Radford Ruether expounds a 'low Christology' which is rooted in the praxis and message of the historical Jesus. She sees Jesus primarily as proclaimer and practitioner of liberation, one who in his life, death and ministry, proclaims and enacts God's preferential option for the poor and oppressed. Ruether argues: 'Once the mythology about Jesus as Messiah or divine *Logos*, with its traditional masculine imagery, is stripped off, the Jesus of the synoptic Gospels can be recognised as a figure remarkably compatible with feminism. This is not to say, in an anachronistic sense, that "Jesus was a feminist", but rather that the criticism of religious and social hierarchy characteristic of the early portrait of Jesus is remarkably parallel to feminist criticism' (1983, p. 135). Ruether goes on to describe 'Jesus as liberator' as one who 'calls for a renunciation, a dissolution, of the web of status relationships by which societies have defined privilege and deprivation' (1983, p. 137). His authority as liberator 'does not reside in his maleness but in the fact that he has renounced this system of domination and seeks to embody in his person the new humanity of service and mutual empowerment' (*ibid.*). Indeed, Ruether speaks of the 'kenosis of patriarchy', the emptying of patriarchy of its power and prestige, which Jesus accomplishes because of the way in which he lives and proclaims a 'new humanity' 'through a lifestyle that discards the hierarchical caste privilege and speaks on behalf of the lowly' (*ibid.*).

The emphasis on Jesus as prophet of liberation is evident also in much third-world feminist theology. For example, Filipino theologian Virginia Fabella affirms that 'a liberational, hope-filled, love-inspired, and praxis-oriented christology is what holds meaning for me. In the person and praxis of Jesus are found the grounds of our liberation from all oppression and discrimination: whether political or economic, religious or cultural, or based on gender, race or ethnicity' (Fabella and Parks, 1989, p. 10).

Such low Christologies beg the question of Jesus' uniqueness, and theologians like Ruether do not ascribe to a high doctrine of Jesus' divinity. Jesus is seen as a representative human being, one who, like other great teachers, mystics and healers, can hold our humanity before God, as well as reveal the capacity of humanity itself to mediate and incarnate divinity.

Wisdom Christologies: Christ as Sophia

A number of feminist theologians, notably Elisabeth Schüssler Fiorenza (1983, 1995) and Elizabeth Johnson (1992), have developed wisdom Christologies which reclaim and reinterpret Christ through the female figure of Sophia. This ancient biblical tradition of a female Wisdom figure who was with God before the dawn of creation and mediated between humanity and God was, indeed, influential in the earliest Christian thinking about Christ, but the female symbolic significance of Sophia was lost and suppressed by the male Logos tradition. Feminist theologians seek to reclaim the suppressed female wisdom tradition, with its emphasis on holistic, embodied knowledge over the disembodied rationality of Logos. Thus Fiorenza names Jesus 'Sophia's prophet', one who proclaimed the vision of the *basileia* (Kingdom or reign) of God and inaugurated a discipleship of equals in an inclusive, non-hierarchical pattern of community that challenged and threatened the Roman patriarchal order. Johnson speaks of Jesus-Sophia as Wisdom made flesh, the compassionate presence of God in the words and deeds of Jesus, who, in the resurrection, rises again in unimaginable ways and cannot be overcome. Personified Wisdom, which was incarnate in Jesus, is at work all over the world, in many different traditions, manifesting herself in many different forms, both male and female, and so the exclusive male hegemony of Christian tradition is broken and subverted. In the biblical tradition, Wisdom has a strong cosmic role, since she is not confined to the human or earthly realm, but is at work in the whole of the cosmos bringing harmony and cosmic redemption. Some ecofeminists such as Anne Primavesi (1991) reclaim this cosmic dimension of the wisdom tradition to speak of Christ as a kind of Eco-Sophia who reconciles earth and humanity and puts the redemption of creation at the centre of Christological concern. We also find some interesting examples of wisdom christologies emanating from diverse contemporary cultural contexts, such as Ji-Sun

Kim's (2001) proposal to interpret Christ through the lens of the Buddhist notion of prajna.

Relational Christologies: Christ as erotic connection

Where wisdom Christologies look to interpret the presence and activity of Christ through the presence and activity of Sophia throughout all time and places, other feminist theologians draw on the notion of eros and relationality to interpret the person and work of Christ. Rita Nakashima Brock (1988) and Carter Heyward (1982, 1984) speak of Christ as erotic power, located not exclusively or even primarily in the historical Jesus, but in 'Christic community', which is evident wherever right relationships of mutuality and justice are operating. Why name this power of connection erotic? Brock and Heyward speak of the erotic, not in a narrowly sexual sense, but as a type of embodied, incarnational and passionate love that seeks for connection and right relation between persons, between God and humanity, between God, humanity and the cosmos. This erotic power of connection is exemplified in the life of Jesus, who healed by touch and created a community of mutuality around him, but the Christic power of connection cannot be limited to the historical Jesus. It is the creative power of God that seeks and longs for connection, and, in connecting, heals the dualism and separation that is the source of the world's injustice and pain. By employing the language of eros and passion, such Christologies seek to reclaim the body and the senses as positive and as the locus of the divine, and, at the same time, to make the connection between the personal and the political, for, as Heyward insists, there can be no right relation without justice, and the passion which drives towards connection between lovers also yearns for well-being in the wider created order.

Womanist Christologies: Jesus as co-sufferer, healer and provider

The philosophical speculations of white feminist theology, with its questioning of the classical doctrinal formulations about Christ and its attempts to reformulate them, have been remote from most black Christian women's experience and concerns. Jacquelyn Grant's (1989) stinging critique of feminist Christology asserted that much white reflection on Jesus had been racist, and had ignored race and class oppression. Womanist Christologies, such as those developed by Grant, Kelly Brown Douglas (1994) and others, are rooted in multidimensional analyses of women's oppression, as well as in black women's experience of Jesus, which has tended to be very different from that of white women. In the womanist tradition, Jesus is affirmed as God made real, the one who 'brings God down to earth' (Douglas, 1996, p. 38) as the actual presence of God in the daily lives of African-American women. Christ is seen as a friend and confidant, a co-sufferer who shares and bears women's pain, and a healer and provider as well as a liberator. Such Christologies are strongly concrete and contextual, rooted in the traditions of black women in slavery and poverty, and calling on Christ as the power and the compassion of God to resist and to overcome oppression. In such traditions, Jesus may be named as ancestor, one who is ever-present in the very earth, enshrining the values and strengths of black people (Thislethwaite, 1989); as shaman, the healer who rescues and heals women from 'han', the overwhelming sense of impasse, powerlessness and unexpressed resentment and anger which Korean women theologians have described as the prevailing feeling amongst Korean people (Chung Hyun Kyung, 1991); even as bread and grain, that which is humble and of the earth, that which sustains life and body for hungry people, God who is known and tasted in every bite of food, whose eucharistic presence is made known not only in the bread of the sacrament, but in the bread of daily life and in the bread of struggle and toil.

EXERCISE

Choose one or two of the Christological models or titles developed by feminist theologians – Christ as Wisdom, Christ as Liberator, Christ as Erotic Power, and so on. Write a piece in the first person, in the voice of Christ or Christa, expressing what you see to be the key aspects of the particular Christological model. For example, 'I am Christ Sophia. I am the source of all Wisdom, wherever it is to be found' and so on. What new insights emerge for you?

Further reading

Daly, M (1985), *Beyond God the Father: toward a philosophy of women's liberation*, London, Women's Press, chapter 3.

Hampson, D (1990), *Theology and Feminism*, Oxford, Blackwell, chapter 2.

Isherwood, L (2001), *Introducing Feminist Christologies*, Sheffield, Sheffield Academic Press.

Parsons, S F (ed.) (2002), *The Cambridge Companion to Feminist Theology*, Cambridge, Cambridge University Press, chapter 9.

Ruether, R R (1983), *Sexism and God-Talk*, London, SCM, chapter 5.

Stevens, M (1993), *Reconstructing the Christ Symbol: essays in feminist christology*, New York, Paulist Press.

6. CAN REDEMPTION BE REDEEMED? SALVATION AND ATONEMENT IN FEMINIST PERSPECTIVE

Introduction

At the heart of Christianity is the claim that, in the life, death and resurrection of Jesus Christ, God has acted decisively to save the world from the catastrophic effects of sin, and to deliver humanity and creation from bondage. From New Testament times onward, there have been a variety of understandings of Christ's atoning work, drawing on diverse metaphors to explain what was happening in Christ's death on the cross and how it effected salvation. Dominant theories of atonement include the ransom theory, in which Christ's death is understood as the ransom paid to release prisoners from sin; the satisfaction theory, in which Jesus' death is regarded as the vicarious sacrifice required to satisfy the wrath of God against sin; the 'Christus Victor' theory, in which Christ is seen as a conquering hero who descended to hell to defeat the powers of evil; and the moral influence theory, in which the life, death and resurrection of Jesus are regarded as powerful demonstrations of the love of God which draw hearers to repentance and thereby to salvation. The church has never officially sanctioned any one understanding of atonement, though there has always been a close focus on the death of Christ as the locus of atonement, the cross being understood not simply as an historical accident brought about by the actions of men, but as central to the divine plan and as theologically necessary to repair the ravages of sin and effect salvation.

Classic atonement theories have given rise to endless debate in modern times and have been widely critiqued from all quarters. Much of the New Testament imagery appears alien if not positively repulsive to contemporary hearers; and, in addition, traditional explanations of the atonement can seem to drive a wedge between God the Father who sends his son to save the world and requires his death, and God the Son who willingly offers up his life as a sacrifice to satisfy the Father.

Feminists share in some of this general dis-ease but, in addition, voice specific concerns about the effects of atonement theories upon women's psychological, spiritual and physical well-being, and charge that the cross of Christ, far from 'saving' women from sin and evil, has been used throughout Christian history to justify and legitimise women's suffering and victimisation. We consider such critiques below, before going on to look at alternative feminist approaches to the death of Christ and redemption.

Reflecting on experience

What does 'redemption' or 'salvation' mean to you? Do such notions have common currency in our society, or are they merely outdated theological jargon?

Consider what you have been taught, or picked up, about the death of Christ. Why was it necessary? What does it demonstrate or achieve?

Feminist critiques of redemption and atonement

Feminist discussion of redemption has ranged widely around the whole question of salvation, its meaning and scope and how it relates to the Christ-event. There has also been intense debate around the death of Christ and Christian understandings of atonement focused in the cross. Here, we shall focus mostly on this second, more localised debate, without ignoring completely wider considerations. Feminist critique has raised profound questions about the death orientation of Christian atonement theories, the model of Christ as a saving victim and its effects on women, and the whole notion of a suffering God.

Atonement: a necrophiliac obsession?

Traditional atonement theories have focused on the *death* of Christ as the locus of God's saving act and much of Christian worship and iconography focuses on the cross as an object of worship. The bleeding, dying man is offered as a potent symbol of God. Some feminists critique such a fixation on death and death symbolism, regarding it as a morbid, necrophiliac obsession rooted in male fear of personal extinction and jealousy of women's capacity to create life, which legitimates violence and war-mongering. Mary Grey questions the impact of Christianity's death symbolism on the behaviour and attitudes of those who imbibe it in worship and preaching and internalise it at a profound level: 'as Christianity has now had two thousand years of death symbolism, it is at least *possible* that the slaughter perpetrated in the name of Christendom is related to its symbols of death, blood-guilt and sacrifice, and that an *alternative* way of encapsulating the redemptive events might stimulate more compassionate lifestyles' (Grey, 1989, p. 139).

Feminists also point out the irony in the fact that Christianity has laid such stress on the blood of Jesus, shed in a violent death, as cleansing, healing and life-giving, when the blood of women, shed in menstruation and in birth-giving, has been seen as dirty, dangerous and profane. Gabrielle Dietrich expresses the outrage of many women at this contradiction in a powerful poem (in Kyung, 1991, p. 69):

> I am a woman
> and the blood
> of my sacrifices
> cries out to the sky
> which you call heaven.
> I am sick of you priests
> who have never bled
> and yet say:
> This is my body
> given up for you
> and my blood
> shed for you
> drink it.
> Whose blood
> has been shed
> for life
> since eternity?

Christ's atoning body and blood, celebrated in the eucharist, have effectively displaced the flesh and blood bodies of women and, far from effecting an attitude of reverence and respect for women's bodies, have legitimised the fear of female flesh.

Christ as saving victim: the divine child abuser?
In atonement theories, the death of Christ is atoning precisely because it is the death of an innocent, sinless victim who did not deserve to die

but whose death and suffering was offered *on behalf of* others to atone for their sin. Thus in Christianity, the innocent suffering of the victim comes to be seen as something noble and inherently redemptive; something that Christians are encouraged to emulate in their own lives. This, when allied with the strong stress on redemption as a free gift of God which human beings can do nothing to effect but can only receive, can reinforce women's powerlessness and oppression and encourage them to see their suffering as God-given and willed. It leads to the adoption of the role of victim and martyr, which, in the powerless, merely reinforces lack of self-worth. It reinforces, so some have argued, the tendency in women to regard ourselves as the 'other' for whom Christ died, and encourages us to look to a male God for salvation, rather than seeking to take responsibility for our own lives. Thus Daly asserts, 'the qualities that Christianity idealises, especially for women, are also those of the victim: sacrificial love, passive acceptance of suffering, humility, meekness' (Daly, 1986, p. 77). In similar vein, Joanne Carlson Brown and Rebecca Parker (1989, p. 3) suggest that 'Christian theology with atonement at the center . . . encourages martyrdom and victimization'.

The critique goes further. Because some atonement theories teach that God the Father actually *required* the death of his own son, a sadomasochistic pattern is set up within the very godhead, according to some feminists, and this perpetuates and legitimises the worst kind of abuse – physical, sexual and psychological – of women and children and other oppressed groups. Thus Brown and Parker claim that 'Christianity has been a primary – in many women's lives *the* primary – force in shaping our acceptance of abuse . . . Divine child abuse is paraded as salvific and the child who suffers "without even raising a voice" is lauded as the hope of the world' (1989, p. 2). Rita Nakashima Brock (1989, p. 52) makes a similar case:

> [Christian] doctrines of salvation reflect and support images of benign paternalism, the neglect of children, or, at their worst, child abuse, making such behaviors acceptable as divine behavior – cosmic paternalism, neglect, and child abuse as it were. The father allows, or even inflicts, the death of his only son. The goodness and power of the father and the unworthiness and powerlessness of his children make the father's punishment just and the blame the children's.

Delores Williams (1993) brings a race perspective to the critique of the cross, rooting her analysis in the experience of African-American slave women as surrogate sex objects and arguing that the theology of atonement that makes the innocent sufferings of Jesus on the cross a surrogate for sinful humanity merely reinforces unjust suffering, particularly the surrogate suffering of black women. The cross 'is the image of human sin in its most desecrated form' (1993, p. 166), not a means of redemption.

A suffering God: how salvific for women?

The restatement of atonement in more 'acceptable' terms in contemporary theologies of a suffering God who suffers in and with 'his' creation does not, according to Brown and Parker, alleviate the problem, for such theologies still hold up suffering as essentially redemptive and thereby encourage the acceptance of suffering on the part of those who suffer unjustly:

> The Suffering God theologies continue in a new form the traditional piety that sanctions suffering as imitation of the holy one. Because God suffers and God is good, we are good if we suffer. If we are not suffering, we are not good. To be like God is to take on the pain of all ... The glorification of anyone's suffering allows the glorification of all suffering. To argue that salvation can only come through the cross is to make God a divine sadist and a divine abuser.
>
> (Brown and Parker, 1989, pp. 19, 23)

These are strong, even shocking, claims, and not all feminists share this condemnation of the cross and of the notion of a suffering God, as we shall see below. Whatever we make of them, they are certainly serious claims and not to be brushed aside lightly.

EXERCISE

'Creating an understanding of atonement that does not posit a need for the suffering or death of anyone but that does respond to the daily reality of earthly suffering, death and ordinary brokenness may well be one of the greatest challenges facing feminist theology today' (Tatman, 1996, p. 12). How far do you agree?

The effects: salvation in the here or the hereafter?

Whilst much feminist critique of atonement theory has focused on the death of Christ, wider discussion of the meaning of redemption has also taken place. In particular, feminists have critiqued the strong future and other-worldly orientation of much classic Christian thought. Throughout Christian tradition, from New Testament times onwards, there has been a conflict between two basic models of redemption which we might describe as individualistic, spiritualised and other-worldly on the one hand, versus social, incarnational and this-worldly on the other. Influenced by Platonic ideas, the first tradition sees redemption essentially as reconciliation of the individual sinner with God and escape from the conditions of mortal existence, including bodiliness, finitude, history and time, into a heavenly world that is our destination and home. This tradition sees present, historical reality and the created order itself as, finally, no more than a 'vale of soul-making'; history itself is not the locus of redemption, and the world can be abandoned to its own unregenerate ways. In this tradition, women are identified with all that is sinful and unregenerate: the body, the passions, matter itself, chaotic and uncontrollable nature – and, in order to be redeemed, women must subjugate their bodies and passions to the rule of (masculine) reason and religious authority. Feminist theology, along with other liberationist approaches, strongly critiques this other-worldly notion of redemption for its neglect of the social conditions of the oppressed, its passive acceptance of the political status quo, and its negation of the body, matter and creation itself.

EXERCISE

Visit your nearest local art gallery or museum which has a good collection of religious art – or find some books of religious art in your local library – and make a study of pictures of the crucifixion from different periods of Christian history. Alternatively, make a study of a selection of Christian hymns about the death of Christ.

- What kind of image of Christ is portrayed, and what does this convey about the love, wrath and justice of God?
- How is suffering depicted? What is the implicit theology of suffering represented by the picture (or hymn)? What message does it give to those who suffer?
- Where, if at all, are women in portrayals of the cross? What roles do they play? What responses do they make to the suffering of Christ? What does this convey about women's place in the Christian scheme of things?

Feminist approaches to atonement

Feminist critiques of atonement are trenchant and not to be lightly or quickly rectified. Nevertheless, feminist theologians also offer some constructive ways forward in thinking about the meaning of redemption and atonement, and in reinterpreting the saving work of Christ. Generally, these interpretations are marked by a broadening out of the notion of redemption away from a transaction located in the cross of Christ, a reclamation of the whole incarnation as redemptive, and an insistence on a this-worldly, communal and justice-oriented notion of redemption.

Atonement as at-one-ment, redemption as right relation

Feminist theologians such as Carter Heyward (1982, 1984) and Mary Grey (1989) have sought to reclaim atonement as a broad, life-oriented process of reconciliation and at-one-ment which is shared between God and humanity. This approach emphasises redemption as a process of coming into right relation with self, other and God, via the claiming of an authentic selfhood and the exercise of justice-making relations with others against all that threatens to disrupt love and justice in the world. The passion of God is understood as God's total commitment to and involvement in the whole creation, of which the life and death of Jesus is a, or perhaps the, prime exemplar of right relation, but is not the only one. For Carter Heyward, redemption is not about waiting for deliverance but about becoming friends and co-creators with God/ess in a co-redemptive process, in which human beings take responsibility for creating right relation through justice and love, here and now, on the earth. 'Instead of a "once-for-all" action performed by a faraway God atonement necessarily becomes a theory concerning what it means to live in a faithful community as one person among many, one community among many; even, from an ecological perspective, one species among many' (Tatman, 1996, p. 12). In such an approach there is no particular focus on the *death* of Jesus as the locus of atonement. Whilst the cross may exemplify the cost of living redemptively, and may even exemplify in a special way the relational love of God, it must not be isolated from the wider life and ministry of Jesus. 'What is redeeming is not Jesus' sufferings and death, but his life, his vision of justice and right relation restored in communities of celebration and abundant life' (Ruether, 1998, p. 102). Theologians such as Heyward and Grey emphasise the need to abandon a Christocentrism which places the death of

Jesus centre-stage and to understand redemption as a shared, co-operative work between God and humanity, in which humans do not passively receive salvation but take responsibility for creating right relation here and now.

The death of Christ reinterpreted

If the death of Christ is not the locus of redemption, and is not, in itself, atoning, how is it to be understood? Is it a wholly pernicious symbol supporting suffering and abuse, or can it have positive meanings for women today? Whilst some feminists reject the cross as a patriarchal image which valorises oppression and abuse, other feminists believe it can be reclaimed as a positive symbol and offer a variety of ways of re-reading the cross. For many, it is **the paradigmatic example of what happens to those who fight against injustice.** In this approach, the death of Jesus is seen as neither essential nor salvific *per se*. Rather, the cross is a tragic but authentic example of what happens to those who fight against injustice. According to Fiorenza (1995), the Sophia-God of Jesus does not demand or need atonement or sacrifice; Jesus' death is not willed by God but is the result of his all-inclusive praxis as the prophet of Sophia. Jesus takes his commitment to liberation to its costly conclusion, facing and accepting death as the price to be paid for standing out against injustice and for freedom. The basileia or sacred community of Jesus' disciples came into being when the women who remained at the cross resisted being broken apart by the destruction and violence they witnessed. The cross thus becomes an empowering force for resistance and this is its redemptive power. For Williams, the cross needs to be recognised as a symbol of evil, an extreme example of the risk taken by anyone struggling for liberation against systems of domination. For Dorothee Sölle (1995), the cross is the ultimate expression of the retaliation of the mighty powers of religion and state against Jesus' demand for justice. Redemption happens when we resist and reject collaboration with injustice and unmask the systems of evil, such as those that put Jesus on the cross and that continue to sacrifice and mutilate people today.

For others, **the cross of Jesus exemplifies the co-suffering of God with and alongside all those who suffer, particularly women.** In the cross, God intentionally stands alongside and identifies with the unjust sufferings and abuse of women. As such, the cross is not a model of how suffering is to be born but a call to radical love and the witness to God's desire that no one should have to suffer again. We remember the cross not to *repeat* it but precisely as the judgement upon all human victimisation and violence, God's final word against all scapegoating. The cross can then be understood as an empowering memory which strengthens contemporary Christians to resist unjust suffering and abuse. This notion of a co-suffering God has been and continues to be particularly significant to womanist, mujerista and minjung theologians. Thus Jacquelyn Grant asserts, 'The living memory of a co-suffering God who knows what it is to be oppressed and whipped and killed by the "masters" has been and continues to be an incredibly powerful source of strength and resistance and hope to many black women' (1989). Chung Hyung Kyung comments, 'Making meaning out of suffering is a dangerous business . . . yet Jesus takes sides with the silenced Asian woman in his solidarity with all oppressed people. This Jesus is Asian women's lover, comrade and suffering servant' (1991, pp. 55–56). This emphasis on the cross as God co-suffering with women is also expressed very strongly in the Christa figure, which, for many women, expresses at a profound level the utter identification of God with female bodily suffering and victimisation. By inhabiting and sharing women's pain, God empowers women to find healing from their sufferings.

Another approach paradoxically emphasises the death of Christ as **a bringing to birth, the locus of a new creation**, calling upon birth imagery to reinterpret the redemptive work of Christ. Parallels are drawn between the suffering and labour of a woman bringing to birth and the suffering and labour of Jesus on the cross. In both cases, the suffering is real, costly and bloody, but it is suffering in the service of life, not death, and it issues in a new creation. This approach has roots in medieval mysticism, particularly in Julian of Norwich's reading of Jesus as the Mother who brings to birth and nourishes his children by his body and blood. Sara Maitland writes graphically of the labour of Christ on the cross in terms of a woman's birth pangs, and suggests that 'the creative birthing of God as expressed in Christ's passion . . . can be given a deeper relating if we can learn to hear as holy the bodily experiences of women, and trust the metaphor of God the Mother' (in Loades, 1990, p. 154). Gabriele Dietrich (2001) compares the sacrificial blood of Jesus on the cross to women's menstrual blood, which is the guarantee of the possibility of life and the continual renewal of life. In a blessing to be said over bread and wine, she unites the shed blood of Jesus with the shed blood of women and sees both as calling for the preservation and redemption of all life:

The blood of Jesus and the blood of women
shed together
tells us to work for the life of the world.
(Dietrich, 2001, pp. 145–146)

The cross is, perhaps, a more mysterious and multi-faceted symbol than some feminists have allowed, and may be capable of restatement in positive ways. As Elisabeth Moltmann-Wendel (in Fiorenza, 1995, p. 99) has suggested,

> In the last analysis, the cross is a paradoxical symbol. It is not simply the guillotine or the gallows. It is also subconsciously the symbol of wholeness and life and it probably could only survive as a central Christian symbol because of this simultaneous subconscious meaning.

EXERCISE
How do you rate the different attempts to create a new atonement theology described above? Choose one of these approaches, and write a poem or narrative in response to it, or try painting the image of redemption it suggests.

Redemption in time and history

If redemption is essentially about right relation, about justice between persons, groups, society, humanity and the earth, then it is something that has to be located primarily in the here-and-now, in time and history. Feminist theology, in common with all liberation movements, emphasises the gospel imperative to work for the conditions of God's reign in the present, and not simply to look for it in the future. It is also an inclusive vision which stretches far beyond gender justice, though that is fundamental. It looks for the breaking down of every dualism and injustice, and for the creation of a state of 'shalom' that includes every creature, nonhuman as well as human. Redemption is for the whole cosmos, not simply for the human realm. Ecofeminism emphasises the essential link between the redemption of women and the redemption of the earth. Of course, feminist theology recognises a future dimension to redemption; the right relation for which it longs and works remains a long way off. Yet this is not a cause for pessimism so much as a spur to renewed vision and action. And the future envisaged by feminism remains a real historical future, not heaven or some mythical time beyond history: redemption is a real historical possibility that is in our hands as well as in the heart and desire of God. For this reason, as well as others, many feminists do not set much store by the notion of personal immortality. Traditional notions of life after death are rejected as a denial of finitude and the egotistical longing to preserve the self at any expense. Rather, for many feminists, an authentic ecological spirituality entails the embrace of one's own mortality and the pursuit of a communal future in which one's own personal destiny finds meaning in something much bigger, the ongoing life of the whole cosmos. The concrete content of feminist hope is well expressed in a Women's Creed written by Robin Morgan for the Fourth International Women's Conference held in Bejing in 1995:

> Bread. A clean sky. Active peace. A woman's voice singing somewhere. The army disbanded. The harvest abundant. The wound healed. The child wanted. The prisoner freed. The body's integrity honoured. The lover returned . . . Labor equal, fair and valued. No hand raised in any gesture but greeting. Secure interiors – of heart, home and land – so firm as to make secure borders irrelevant at last. (in Ruether, 1998, p. 120)

Thus feminist theologians share an ultimately optimistic vision, both of the human capacity to effect justice and right relation in the earth, and of God's longing for the world.

EXERCISE
Consider Robin Morgan's vision of future redemption. How far do you think it approximates to Christian hope? Where is God in it? Try writing your own version.

Further reading

Brown, J C and Bohn, C R (eds) (1989), *Christianity, Patriarchy and Abuse: a feminist critique*, New York, Pilgrim Press.

Daly, M (1985), *Beyond God the Father: toward a philosophy of women's liberation*, London, Women's Press.

Fiorenza, E Schüssler (1995), *Jesus: Miriam's child, Sophia's prophet*, London, SCM, chapter 4.

Grant, J (1989), *White Women's Christ and Black Women's Jesus*, Atlanta, Scholars Press.

Grey, M (1989), *Redeeming the Dream: feminism, redemption and Christian tradition*, London, SPCK.

Kyung, C H (1991), *Struggle to Be the Sun Again*, London, SCM.

Ruether, R R (1998), *Introducing Redemption in Christian Feminism*, Sheffield, Sheffield Academic Press.

7. THE HOLY SPIRIT AS THE FEMININE IN GOD? PNEUMATOLOGY IN FEMINIST PERSPECTIVE

Introduction

In Christian tradition, the Spirit is the mysterious yet dynamic agency of God in creation and redemption, the power and the presence of God, the one who mediates God to the world. As such, the Spirit *is* God and shares in the Trinitarian life of the Father and the Son in co-equal mutuality (though the western church, from the Council of Constantinople onwards, has tended to subordinate the Spirit to the other two persons of the Trinity). At its most basic, the Spirit is breath or wind, that which gives and sustains life. Thus God the Spirit is both creator and recreator, the One who gives life moment by moment to everything that exists and holds the creation in being. The Spirit is the energy, the inspiration and the impulse to life and to justice, the source of all truth and the continuation of the presence and mission of Jesus in the world.

In contrast to the dominant biblical metaphors and models for God and Christ, which are largely masculine, the central biblical metaphors for the Spirit – *ruah* (wind, breath), *shekinah* (presence, dwelling) and *hokmah* or *sophia* (wisdom) – are either female or gender non-specific, and are often drawn from the natural, rather than the human realm. In scripture, the Spirit is breath, wind and flame rather than personified in human images. On the surface, there might seem to be fewer problems, then, for feminists in engaging with Christian discourse about the Spirit, since the dominant understandings of Spirit are not male, and there is more potential for a feminist understanding of the person and work of the Holy Spirit. Certainly there appear to be solid biblical grounds for naming the Spirit as female, and one can point to examples of such naming at different periods of Christian tradition, even if this has been a marginal and largely repressed tradition. Yet Christian doctrine about the Spirit (technically known as pneumatology, the study of the Spirit) is by no means unproblematic for feminists, as we shall consider below. Nevertheless, feminist theologians are engaged in the creative enterprise of reclaiming and renewing theology of the Spirit in our time, and we shall look at some examples of feminist approaches to the Spirit, before going on in chapter 9 to consider what this might mean in terms of the practice of spirituality – a closely related area.

Reflecting on experience

What image or images come to mind when you think of the Holy Spirit?

Do you think of the Spirit as male, female or neither?

Do you find it liberating or problematic that the Spirit cannot be captured in human, anthropomorphic, terms?

A feminist problematising of pneumatology

Feminists draw attention to the ways in which the work and person of the Spirit have been neglected, subordinated and institutionalised within Christian tradition, and the oppressive results this has had for women.

The neglect of the Spirit in western tradition

The first problem highlighted by feminists is simply the fact that the Spirit has been much neglected and marginalised in western theology, thus reinforcing the dominance of the male in Christian God-language. Elizabeth Johnson (1992, p. 130) notes the variety of metaphors employed by contemporary theologians to express this neglect of the Spirit: the Spirit is imaged as 'faceless' (Walter Kasper), 'shadowy' (John Macquarrie), 'ghostly' (Georgia Harkness); or 'anonymous', the 'poor relation' in the Trinity (Norman Pittinger); the 'unknown' or 'half-known' God (Yves Congar); in Johnson's own phrase, the Spirit is the 'forgotten God'. This neglect of the Spirit is also reflected in Christian art, where the Spirit is usually portrayed as a dove, both in images of the Trinity and in events associated with the incarnation of Jesus, such as the annunciation, baptism and crucifixion. In such depictions, the Spirit often appears somewhat incidental to the proceedings, a cipher and a travesty of divine power.

Feminists reflect on both the *causes* and the *effects* of this neglect of the Spirit in Christian self-understanding. They speculate that it may not be accidental that the Spirit in biblical understanding is referred to in female terms; just as all female traditions have been repressed and marginalised in Christianity, so the Spirit herself was pushed out and her close association with the feminine repressed and ignored. This had the effect of maintaining the dominance of patriarchal thought-forms and ways in Christian understanding – crudely, the male Father and the Son maintained the power over the female Spirit – and of keeping women's experience marginal and repressed. The hiddenness, anonymity and invisibility of women was mirrored and reflected in the facelessness and namelessness of the Spirit in Christian worship, theology and life.

The subordination of the Spirit

Not only has the Spirit been neglected in western tradition, but, when given serious theological consideration, has often been subordinated to the Father and the Son, a kind of Cinderella of the Trinity – and this, according to feminists, has justified and legitimised women's sub-ordination to men in the private, social and ecclesial domain. The Spirit seems always to have taken 'third place', nearly always treated in systematic theologies only after a full account has been given of divine creation and redemption. Johnson (1992, p. 128) speculates on the reasons for this:

> Perhaps the understanding of Spirit receives such short shrift due to this placement itself, coming at the end when a great deal about divinity and God's ways with the world has already been explicitly discussed. Perhaps, especially in the West, the neglect is due to the nature of the thought systems that emphasize divine transcendence in a less than relational way. Perhaps toward the end of their long constructive treatises theologians simply got tired.

Dominant western notions of the Spirit have reinforced her subordination. For example, Augustine's notion of the Spirit as the bond of love between the Father and the Son, restated in modern times by the likes of John V Taylor in his metaphor of the 'Go-Between God' (Taylor, 1972), reinforces the anonymity of the Spirit. For in such models, the Spirit is not valued in her own right so much as the mediator between the two dominant persons, the Father and the Son. When the mediator is also female, this also reinforces women's classic role as the reconciler, the restorer of difficult relationships, the go-between in human affairs who is self-effacing and looks only to keep the peace between the menfolk.

After the Reformation, Protestant theology tended to privatise the range of the Spirit's activity, limiting it to the work of justification and sanctification of the individual believer, while post-Tridentine Catholic theology displaced the Spirit's work on to Mary or the pope or the cult of the Blessed Sacrament, thus institutionalising it. In both cases, the Spirit's activity and presence became both hidden and subordinated, as well as drastically curtailed.

The regulation and control of the Spirit by the church

In the Bible, the Spirit is the free, mysterious presence and power of God that moves without hindrance or let over the whole creation. In John's Gospel, Jesus compares the Spirit to the wind, which 'blows where it chooses, and you hear the sound of it, but you do not know where it comes from or where it goes' (John 3:8). In Acts, the Spirit falls on the disciples at Pentecost without warning and is symbolised in tongues of fire and in strange tongues of diverse utterance – both images of divine mystery, power and uncontrollability. Yet feminists critique Christian tradition for its attempts to control, institutionalise and limit the free, mysterious work of the Spirit. We have already mentioned above the limitation of the Spirit in post-Reformation Protestant and Catholic theology, albeit this was achieved in different ways. We will see this tendency demonstrated when we look at the history of Christian spirituality and note the ways in which the church attempted to regulate, control and institutionalise the practice of spirituality, often limiting it to the private realm. Sallie McFague (1993, 1996) suggests that there has always been a tension in Christian tradition between a 'broad versus a narrow understanding of divine Spirit' (1996, p. 146). The first sees the Spirit as the life-giving breath of God at work in all creation and all peoples; the second limits the scope of the Spirit's work to the church and those who confess allegiance to Christ, and has attempted to domesticate the Spirit by regulating its activity. This second, more exclusive tradition, has tended to emphasise the work of God in redemption over the Spirit's work in creation, the importance of a 'second birth' over the first, common birth, and has understood Jesus as the one way to God against a universalist understanding of grace.

EXERCISE

Using a concordance, look up references to the Spirit or Holy Spirit in the Bible. Make a list of the images that are used, and consider how many of these images are gender-specific, and how many are drawn from the non-human realm. Now look at some hymns about the Spirit in one or two hymn books, and consider the images of the Spirit that they use. You might also like to look at images of God the Trinity in art, or depictions of the ministry of Christ, and see how the Holy Spirit is portrayed.

- What do you learn from this survey about the ways in which the Spirit has been understood and portrayed?
- Can you find examples of female naming of the Spirit?
- What names or images of the Spirit would you use to draw out the mystery, power and universality of the Spirit's work?

Feminist theologies of the Spirit

How, then, is the Spirit to be spoken of, and how are the person and work of the Spirit to be understood? Feminist theologians are engaged in both retrieving positive aspects of ancient traditions which name the Spirit as female and developing new approaches. We can identify a variety of perspectives.

The Spirit as the feminine dimension in God

Some feminists, as well as others, speak of the Spirit as the feminine dimension in God and name the Spirit in feminine imagery and terms. This approach has ancient roots in early Semitic and Syrian traditions, which took the cue from scriptural female Spirit imagery to speak of the Spirit as the mother who brings to birth Christ in the incarnation, new members of the body of Christ in the waters of baptism, and the body of Christ through the epiclesis of the eucharist. Recent examples of this approach are to be found in Congar's (1983) naming of the Spirit as the feminine person in God, Boff's (1987) alignment of the Spirit with Mary as the maternal face of God, Gelpi's (1984) reappropriation of the feminine archetype in his theology of 'Holy Breath', and Marriage's (1989) notion of the Spirit as 'the mother who lets us go'.

However, as we have already seen in chapter 3, this approach is essentially compensatory and does little to challenge the balance of masculine imagery in Christian thought. The overarching framework of such theologies remains androcentric, with the male principle still dominant and sovereign and the third female person or principle subordinate to the male. In addition, the female naming of the Spirit relies on essentialising stereotypes of the feminine, which is variously identified with mothering, affectivity, darkness or virginity. Introducing such a feminine dimension into the Godhead may enlarge traditional understandings of masculinity and thus be helpful to men, but it does little to challenge traditional female roles and rights.

Reconceiving the Spirit within the totality of the Trinity

A more radical approach, represented by theologians such as Johnson and McFague, requires a wholesale reworking of all God-language, not simply the feminisation of the Spirit. These theologians attempt to restate a theology of the Spirit within a wider framework of a reworking of trinitarian theology *per se*. Such an approach is to be distinguished from the naming of feminine traits or dimensions in God; rather, it proposes 'speech about God in which the fullness of female humanity as well as of male humanity and cosmic reality may serve as divine symbol, in equivalent ways' (Johnson, 1992, p. 47). This approach uses female imagery and experience positively to speak of God, but it also uses a wide range of other imagery and experience, both gendered and nongendered, and it seeks to move away from stereotypes of what it means to be male or female, so that the God-language does not simply reinscribe traditional gender roles.

Johnson's impressive study of God-language is a creative example of this approach, in which she attempts a systematic trinitarian theology rooted in women's experience of the Spirit. In contrast to classical theologies which began either with the unity of divine nature or the 'first person' of the Trinity, Johnson takes her starting point from the Spirit, 'God's livingness subtly and powerfully abroad in the world'. Beginning with interpreted experience of the Spirit, Johnson draws on scriptural traditions of Spirit/Shekinah, Wisdom/Sophia and Mother imagery to develop a trinitarian theology of Spirit-Sophia, 'divinity drawing near and passing by'; Jesus-Sophia, 'wisdom made flesh', and Mother-Sophia, 'unoriginate origin'. She speaks of God as Spirit as the 'gracious, furious mystery of God engaged in a dialectic of presence and absence throughout the world' (1992, p. 133). She emphasises the work of the Spirit in vivifying the creation, in renewing and empowering the earth and transforming unjust structures, and in gracing all the world's

religious traditions – not just Christianity – and all inspired persons –
not just Christians. She acknowledges that Spirit may be spoken of in
many names: Friend, Sister, Mother, Grandmother, as well as male
images and images drawn from the natural world. However we name
her, 'relationality is intrinsic to her very being as love, gift and friend',
yet, 'at the same time that she is intrinsically related, the Spirit is essentially free, blowing like the wind where she wills' (p. 148).

Together, these namings of the Sophia God point us towards the
Triune God, mystery of relation who may be spoken of as 'SHE WHO IS',

> the one whose very nature is sheer aliveness, is the profoundly rela-
> tional source of the being of the whole universe, still under historical
> threat. She is the freely overflowing wellspring of the energy of all
> creatures who flourish, and of the energy of all those who resist the
> absence of her flourishing, both made possible by participating in her
> dynamic act. In the power of her being she causes to be. In the strength
> of her love she gives her name as the faithful promise always to be
> there amidst oppression to resist and bring forth. (Johnson, 1992,
> p. 243)

Another example of reworking theology of the Spirit in ways which
call upon both male and female imagery, as well as wider imagery drawn
from the nonhuman world, is Sallie McFague's work in *Models of God*
(1987) and *The Body of God* (1993). The root model McFague offers is
that of the world as the body of God, in opposition to the monarchical
model of God as transcendent King ruling over his world. 'Spirit'
within the terms of this analogy, is to be understood both as breath and
life which animates the world (body), and as Holy Spirit which renews
and directs life towards ever more inclusive love. McFague develops her
approach as a way of speaking about God that is compatible with contemporary scientific understanding of the world and that addresses the
relation of God to the whole world, not simply the human realm.
'Spirit' becomes the major metaphor for understanding the agency of
God within the world, and it is a way of speaking about God which
neither reduces God to the world nor relegates God to another world.
In contrast to Johnson, McFague prefers to maintain gender neutrality
in her speech about the Spirit:

> It may be best that, for once in Christian reflection, we let God be 'it'.
> 'It' (the divine spirit) roams where it will, not focused on the like-
> minded (the fathers and the sons – or even the mothers and the
> daughters), but permeating, suffusing, and energizing the innermost

being of each and every entity in creation in ways unknown and unknowable in our human, personal categories. (McFague, 1993, p. 147)

Accordingly, of McFague's three proposed models of God, only one, Mother, is specifically female, whilst the other two – Lover and Friend – may be male or female. McFague develops these models in creative and challenging ways as models, not of the relation between God and the individual, but as ways of thinking about the relation between God and the world. To name God as Mother, for example, suggests new ways of envisaging the relation between the universe and God as intimately interconnected, rather than distinct and separate; it suggests a co-dependency and mutuality between God and the world, for to the Mother, the world is offspring, beloved, and companion; and it points to an ethic of justice rooted in the agapic love of the Mother God who affirms the existence of the world which is her body and desires all to share in the fullness of life.

EXERCISE

Consider the following images of the Spirit from different times and places and critically evaluate what they say about divinity and about femaleness.

She [the Spirit] is God in the world, moving, stirring up, revealing, interceding. It is she who calls out, sanctifies, and animates the church. Hers is the water of one baptism. The debt of sin is wiped away by her. She is the life-giver who raises men [sic] from the dead with the life of the coming age. Jesus himself left the earth so that she, the intercessor, might come. (Williams, in Johnson, 1992, pp. 84–85)

And for all this, nature is never spent:
   There lives the dearest freshness deep down things;
And though the last lights off the black West went
   Oh, morning, at the brown brink eastward, springs –
Because the Holy Ghost over the bent
   World bends with warm breast and with ah! bright wings.
(Gerard Manley Hopkins)

The part played in our upbringing by the Holy Spirit is that of a mother – a mother who enables us to know our Father, God, and our brother, Jesus . . . He (the Spirit) teaches us how to practise the virtues and how to use the gifts of a son of God by grace. All this is part of a mother's function. (Congar, 1983, vol. 3, p. 161)

Spirit-Sophia, friend, sister, mother, and grandmother of the world builds relationships of solidarity, not antithesis, between God and human beings and among human beings with each other and the earth. Held in her affection, human beings are called to be genuine companions of all creatures, advocating justice and partnering life, while not being diminished or overpowered by a dominating will. (Johnson, 1992, p. 136)

Reconceiving the Spirit beyond Christian and Eurocentric boundaries

Both Johnson and McFague emphasise the universality and inclusiveness of the Spirit's work – and this is, indeed, a strong theme in much feminist pneumatology. The Spirit is the presence and activity of God in all creation, in all time and place, not simply in the lives or the affairs of those who acknowledge God or Christ. Another strong emphasis is on the this-worldly, earthly presence of the Spirit; the Spirit is immanent, near all life, close to human affairs, not separated from the creation in transcendence. The Spirit is God working to empower and transform the whole creation, to kindle life and to sustain it, especially against the forces of injustice and oppression that would crush life and hope.

All of these emphases can be seen in the work of Korean theologian Chung Hyung Kyung, particularly as exemplified in her 1991 presentation to the World Council of Churches assembly at Canberra, Australia (Kyung, 1994). This presentation caused a huge stir at the WCC gathering, dividing participants in their reactions by its boldness and its identification of the Spirit with the ancestral spirits of Kyung's native Korea. Drawing very deeply from the 'collective unconscious' of the Korean people and their long traditions of spirituality, Kyung addressed the assembly theme of the Spirit and renewal of the creation. She spoke of her country as 'the land of spirits full of han', that is, anger, bitterness, brokenheartedness and grief that comes about when justice is denied.

She named the wandering, han-ridden spirits of those who have died unjustly as 'icons of the Holy Spirit' and 'agents through whom the Holy Spirit has spoken her compassion and wisdom for life' (1994, p. 391). She then invoked the Spirit in a litany of these han-ridden spirits of the dead, including the dead of Korea and Asia and other parts of the world, victims of the Holocaust and Hiroshima and other massive structural injustices, the murdered 'spirit of the Amazon rainforest', as well as the spirits of the biblical oppressed and prophets of justice such as Jesus and contemporary heroes such as Gandhi, Biko and Malcolm X (1994, pp. 393–394). Her presentation caused such a stir because it challenged the boundaries of much traditional, Eurocentric Christian theology, and refused to limit the Spirit to institutional or religious categories. She identified the work of the Spirit with every struggle towards liberation, making no distinction between the torture and oppression suffered by Jesus and that suffered by the rainforests, women down the ages, and every marginalised group. She aligned herself with a broad, rather than a narrow understanding of the Spirit, and compared the Spirit to the goddess Kwan Yn, venerated as the goddess of compassion and wisdom in the East, who 'can go into nirvana any time she wants to, but refuses to go into nirvana by herself', rather 'wait[ing] and wait[ing] until the whole universe, people, trees, birds, mountains, air, water, become enlightened' (Kyung, 1994, p. 394). She called on all participants to join in the work of the Spirit in breaking down every barrier of injustice and in 'fighting for our life on this earth in solidarity with all living beings, and building communities for justice, peace, and the integrity of creation' (p. 394).

EXERCISE
🕮 **Read the extract** from Chung Hyun Kyung's presentation to the WCC Assembly in *Feminist Theology from the Third World: a reader*, edited by Ursula King (1994). How does this enlarge or challenge your understanding of the Spirit? Try writing your own litany of invocation to the Spirit. What images would you choose to name the Spirit, and why?

Further reading

Coakley, S (1988), 'Femininity' and the Holy Spirit? in M Furlong (ed.), *Mirror to the Church: reflections on sexism*, London, SPCK, pp. 124–135.

Johnson, E (1992), *She Who Is: the mystery of God in feminist theological discourse*, New York, Crossroad, chapter 7.

Kyung, C H (1994), Come, Holy Spirit – break down the walls with wisdom and compasssion, in U King (ed.), *Feminist Theology from the Third World: a reader*, London, SPCK, pp. 392–394.

Marriage, A (1989), *Life-Giving Spirit: responding to the feminine in God*, London, SPCK.

8. IN SEARCH OF A ROUND TABLE: ECCLESIOLOGY IN FEMINIST PERSPECTIVE

Introduction

Rosemary Radford Ruether makes the comment that 'the more one becomes a feminist the more difficult it becomes to go to church' (Ruther, 1983, pp. 193–194) and many feminists would agree with her. Although there are many denominational, cultural and social variations, it is still true to say that the church as a whole is riddled with male-dominated hierarchy and clericalism, patriarchal symbolism and language, and its history and traditions, until very recently, have systematically excluded women. For many women, the experience of going to church week after week is profoundly disempowering as they participate in liturgy which is remote and alien and framed in language that excludes them, listen to sermons which do not address the realities of their lives, receive leadership overwhelmingly if not exclusively at the hands of men, and relate to hierarchical and deeply conservative structures which do not seem to admit of change. The creative and exciting developments in feminist theology which we have been considering in this book can seem a million miles away from the realities of ecclesiastical life. Most clergy and laity have never heard of these ideas and are not interested in them, and in many churches, even the most rudimentary awareness of the women's movement and its challenges seems entirely absent. In the UK, for instance, it is still very common to find churches using exclusive language and upholding patriarchal patterns of family and community life without comment or apparent resistance. While some, perhaps many, feminists have responded by leaving the church entirely and seeking new forms of religious nurture, or giving up on religion altogether, others have formed new expressions of church either within existing institutional structures or independently of them.

This is not to deny the crisis of male (lay) participation and involvement in church life, which some commentators consider a more pressing problem. The feminist critique of church life, as well as positive feminist proposals for the reformation of church life, do not simply concern women. Their focus may be on women's experience and situation, but they are concerned with the wholesale transformation of church life, and this can only benefit the entire Christian community, men as well as women, children as well as adults, black as well as white.

Reflecting on experience

From your own experience of the church, however limited or extensive, consider:

- How involved are women in the life of the church? What are their chief roles and functions?
- How far does the worship and liturgy of the church reflect women's experience and needs?
- How far do women exercise leadership within the church? What access to power and decision-making do they have? What authority do they exercise in church life and how is this authority recognised and authorised?
- What differences do you notice between different church traditions and denominations in their attitudes towards women?

Feminist critique of the church

The church represents a place of pain and denial for feminist-identified women who seek to belong to it, in a number of ways: not only in its liturgical and ministerial practices, its structures and leadership, but also in its denial of women's experience and contribution throughout church history, as well as in its theological self-understanding. Below we consider some of the key features of each of these layers: practice, history and theology.

Critiques of church practice and ministry

Women make up the large majority in the congregations of all Christian denominations, yet until very recently have been denied access to its practices, offices and positions of leadership, as well as opportunities for theological study – and even now, the situation is changing only very slowly. Even where women are permitted to exercise leadership in various denominations, there is still a long way to go before there is genuine parity of representation and decision-making. But it is not only that men dominate all the positions of power in the church. A deeper problem lies in the structure and quality of power-relations between male leaders and lay (largely female) church members, and in the underlying structures that shape church life. This is the problem of clericalism, itself a manifestation of the hierarchical nature of the church, which Ruether identifies as the main problem for women in the church, and the most serious distortion of the church's life. Ruether defines clericalism as 'the separation of ministry from mutual interaction with community and its transformation into hierarchically ordered castes of clergy and laity' (1985b, p. 75). In this oppressive power relation, 'the clergy monopolize teaching, sacramental action, and administration and turn the community into passive dependants who are to receive these services from the clergy but cannot participate in shaping and defining them themselves' (1985b, p. 75). Clericalism is built upon patriarchy: its basic symbol and mode of relationship is that of an all-knowing father and a helpless child. It is rooted in hierarchical and dualistic thought-forms and in an oppressive practice of power. In many churches, clerical control is firmly maintained in the hands of men by the simple means of refusing admittance of women to the ranks of the ordained; but even in denominations where women have been ordained, the underlying patterns and assumptions of clericalism continue to operate.

According to Ruether, clericalism disempowers people in three main ways: first, in *sacramental life*, all the symbols of the life of the community are alienated from the people and made into magic tools possessed by the clergy through ordination or other forms of authorisation. The eucharist, in particular, is 'rigidly guarded as a clerical reserve and defined as an act that no lay person can validly perform' (1985b, p. 78). More generally, liturgy becomes a means of obfuscation and control, rather than a source of life-giving nourishment and illumination of women's and men's lives. It loses its connection to the body and experience and cannot be owned by lay people. Thus, 'women in contemporary churches are suffering from linguistic deprivation and eucharistic famine. They can no longer nurture their souls in alienating words that ignore or systematically deny their existence. They are starved for the words of life, for symbolic forms that fully and wholeheartedly affirm their personhood and speak truth about the evils of sexism and the possibility of a future beyond patriarchy' (Ruether, 1985b, p. 5). Second, in *education*, clericalism is evident. 'The clergy monopolise theological education, removing it to a place inaccessible to the people' (Ruether, 1985b, p. 81). Theological education is developed in a language unknown to the people – either literally, in a foreign language such as Latin, or else in a learned jargon that most people cannot understand. It becomes a specialised, elitist activity removed from the lives of the people and 'the people are thus made to feel helpless and dependent on the clergy to interpret the scriptures and to analyse theological ideas and symbols' (*ibid.*). Third, in *church administration*, clericalism reigns too, although here there are significant differences between the various denominations. The most hierarchical churches, such as Roman Catholicism, exclude the laity from any effective role in church administration at all. By contrast, Protestant churches usually have structures that provide for elected lay delegates, but the danger here is that, because the dominant models of ministry are still clerical ones, lay people tend to be clericalised and their experience and expertise as lay people ignored.

Critiques of church history

As well as engaging with contemporary church practice, another key focus of feminist ecclesiology has been on the past. Church history, from Eusebius of Caesarea onwards, has essentially been the histories of powerful men, written by men and transmitted by men. As Janet Crawford (1996, p. 27) asserts, 'Although it is certain that the church has always consisted of women and men, historically it has been represented as an institution governed by men and women's participation has generally been marginalized, trivialized, or ignored altogether.' The 'master narrative' of church history as the exploits of powerful men has had a totalising effect that has excluded from its account the experience of ordinary Christians; the Eurocentric focus of the narrative has also excluded many localities from the account, thereby functioning in a racist as well as a sexist way.

The marginalisation of women within church history is reflected in church calendars where women continue to be a minority, despite efforts to improve the ratio of women to men. In an analysis of the then relatively recent Anglican Alternative Service Book, Janet Morley (1984) counted sixty-six men to ten women in its list of lesser saints, and pointed out that 'it is inherently improbable that one sex should be nearly seven times as saintly as the other' (p. 64). Even where women's lives have been remembered, they are frequently presented in ways which simply reinforce patriarchal assumptions and trivialise, or sexualise, women's achievements. Thus Morley notes that the women whose lives are honoured in the ASB calendar are nearly all defined in terms of their sexuality, whereas the men are never so defined. Thus 'The celibate Francis of Assisi is just a "Friar", but Clare is specifically a "Virgin". Josephine Butler is a "Social Reformer, Wife and Mother", while William Wilberforce is simply a "Social Reformer"'. Morley points to a further difference in the way in which women are denied authoritative teaching status: 'Catherine of Siena, Teresa of Avila, and John of the Cross, all learned spiritual writers, are each described as "Mystics", but only the man has the distinction of being called a "Teacher of the Faith". Why the caution about offering women authoritative status?' (Morley, 1984, p. 64). Thus, even where women are included in church history and tradition, they are subjects in a male-defined world rather than objects in their own right; their stories are told to reinforce a model of holiness for women as sexual abstinence or, if such cannot be achieved, devotion to family and to duty, and obedience to church authority. (It is heartening to note that the recent Common Worship has removed these more blatant sexist stereotypes of women in its list of saints, although the male/female ratio is not much better.)

EXERCISE

Without thinking about it too much, take a piece of paper and write down quickly the names of 15 men who have been important in church history, and 15 women. How easy do you find it to make the lists? What does this exercise tell you about the history of the church you have imbibed?

Critiques of traditional ecclesiologies

The patriarchal and androcentric nature of the church is reflected, not only in present practice and past history, but also in the theologies of church which have held sway down the centuries. This is not surprising, given that women have been largely excluded from the exercise of theology. Natalie Watson (2002) analyses a number of major metaphors and models of the church, suggesting that they are full of 'ambiguity and alienation' for women (p. 30). The female image of the church as the 'bride of Christ', far from endorsing women's liberation has tended to suppress it, since it is based on a patriarchal (and heterosexist) model of marriage in which the husband rules over his humble and submissive bride. The model is one of patriarchal ownership and rule, even if the rule is benign, and has been used throughout church history to endorse women's roles as wives, mothers and virgins (betrothed to Christ). Another female image of church, that of Mary as personification of the church, the ideal disciple and the mother of the church, has been equally ambivalent. As an ideal which real women are unable to achieve (the virgin mother), Mary represents disembodied, sexless femininity and the idealised maternal, at once reinforcing women's primary role as mothers and, at the same time, denying women's sexuality and bodiliness. As the 'first disciple' yet without office or ecclesiastical role, Mary reinforces a masculine priesthood from which women are perpetually excluded. The church as the Body of Christ is regarded as a problematic image because it asserts that women can only receive salvation through identification with a male body, and is thus another denial and repression of the female body. The church as Servant which emulates the servant ministry of Christ becomes a problematic image for women when it is co-joined with the feminine image of the church, for it reinforces women's call to service, traditionally rendered as denial of the self – a dangerous model for those who are already in a position of powerlessness. Even more recent models of the church as the People of God or the gathered worshipping community are regarded by Watson as potentially problematic, because the notion of community can be exclusive, denying difference between subjects and assuming an equality between members that does not actually exist.

EXERCISE

Analyse the hymns in one or two hymn books under the 'Church' section.

- What images and metaphors are used for the church?
- Are the images gendered?
- When the church is presented as female, what characteristics and roles are reinforced?
- What are the effects of such images on real women likely to be?

Feminist ecclesiologies

As Susan Ross (2002, p. 224) notes, 'Over the last three decades, feminist theologians have engaged in a multipronged approach to the issues surrounding women, church, sacrament, and worship'. Here we will focus on feminist contributions to practice, history and tradition, and theological thinking about the nature of the church.

New practices of church

At an immediate practical and political level, feminist reaction to the sexism within the church's structures and tradition tends to take one of two forms. First, there are feminists who are committed to staying within the institutional church, working within the existing structures and remaining under the authority of their church leaders, seeking to reform from within by campaigning for the ordination of women, inclusive language in the liturgy, and so on. Second, increasing numbers of feminists feels that it is no longer possible for them to remain in the institutional church, and they have formed alternative grassroots communities – many of them women-only, but some mixed – in which women take full responsibility for liturgy, teaching and the life of the community. In the United States, this 'exodus' movement out of the institutional church to form alternative Christian communities is widely known as 'Womenchurch', which, despite its name, does not or need not mean an exclusively female community, but a community which is 'woman-centred' or 'woman-affirming', in contrast to the per-ceived woman-denying bias of the mainstream churches. Mary Hunt (1996, p. 240) defines Womenchurch as 'a global, ecumenical movement of feminist base communities which gather in sacrament and solidarity to express their religious faith in egalitarian, democratic styles'. In Britain and some other European countries, there is a lively grass-roots movement of such communities, but it tends to operate at the local level, and there is no national network as yet. A range of such projects is described by a World Council of Churches report (WCC, 2001), includ-ing Women Church in Korea, the St Hilda Community in England, and *Conspirando* in Latin America. In practice, many women (and some men) manage to remain within the institutional church at the same time as belonging to such alternative liturgical groups or communities.

Both within the institutional church and outside it, as well as on its fringes, women and feminist-identified men in different groupings are engaged in an energetic pursuit of new ways of being church more in tune with the 'discipleship of equals' (Fiorenza, 1993) practised by Jesus. There has been an extraordinary flowering of feminist liturgy, hymnody and worship practices which, over time, is beginning to have an impact on the worship of the mainstream churches. Although there is much local variation and colour, one can identify certain key characteristics of this feminist church movement. First, there is a strong commitment to non-hierarchical, shared leadership and mutual power-relations. For many groups this means the rejection of any form of ordained leadership and a sharing out of functions. Second, such groups tend to have fluid boundaries across denominational and other lines; there is little concern with doctrinal or ecclesiastical consensus, and the unifying factor is commitment to justice and transformation of the church rather than traditional ecclesiastical loyalties. Third, the liturgy practised by feminist groups tends to be inclusive, experimental and embodied, often with strong roots in women's neglected experience and a commitment to reclaiming and naming that which has been taboo or invisible in official liturgy. Thus, new rites of passage – for menarche, menopause, setting up home, entering into partnerships, same-sex as well as heterosexual – and rites of healing – for abortion, miscarriage, the end of a relationship, rape or domestic violence – are created, and no aspect of human life is considered beyond the scope of prayer and worship. There is also a strong concern with the preservation of life in the wider cosmos, and a celebrating of the natural cycle of seasons. Fourth, women's new worship traditions not only break with the past in focusing on many aspects of life which have previously been denied, they also call on a much wider range of sources than those officially sanctioned by the church, and are thus engaged in a widening of the canon. Scripture and Christian tradition are called upon, but so too are many contemporary and ancient resources which have not been considered normative or authoritative: art and music, women's literature and poetry, ancient symbols of the Goddess, insights and scriptures of other world faiths, and so on. Where scripture and tradition are employed, they are reworked in creative ways both to highlight women's exclusion and victimisation in the past (for example, in litanies mourning the abuse of women recorded in scripture or the persecution of women as witches in the middle ages), and to reclaim women's exercise of faith down the ages (for example, in the retelling and reworking of biblical stories about women and the celebration of women saints and heroines).

Reclaiming of women's church history

Women have always been church, even if that reality has been systematically denied and written out of the records. Feminist historians of Christian tradition are engaged in a rewriting of church history in such a way as to reclaim and restore the centrality of women's lives to the narrative of the church, as well as to challenge androcentric assumptions about what constitutes significant historical action. Fiorenza's (1983) pioneering work in reconstructing early Christian origins has been important in providing historical roots of the present Women-church movement as well as in challenging previous accounts of the early church which assumed that only men were disciples and apostles. Fiorenza finds evidence in early Christian discourses of an egalitarian, anti-patriarchal discipleship of equals which practised inclusive table-fellowship and healing in anticipation of God's basileia, where justice reigns and hunger, poverty and domination are abolished. She argues that women played key roles as apostles, prophets and leaders within this discipleship of equals, and that this egalitarianism was lost as Christianity expanded into the Greco-Roman world and conformed itself to patriarchal social norms. Other feminist historians have examined the role of women in early ascetical and monastic Christianity (e.g. Clark, 1986), and there has been a huge deal of interest in women's religious communities and their leaders in the medieval period. Figures such as Julian of Norwich, Hildegard of Bingen and Teresa of Avila have been the focus of much important work, but feminist historians have also been concerned with the lives of ordinary women. Caroline Bynum's (1982, 1987) research on the gendered meaning of the body in women's religious experience uncovers the many complex layers of women's religious lives, demonstrating how women developed their own distinctive religiosity within the institutional constraints of the time, whilst Clarissa Atkinson (1991) has explored the meaning of motherhood in the medieval period and how it was shaped and influenced by changing understandings of Mary, the incarnation and the saints. Work on the Reformation period has re-evaluated the meaning for women's lives of the great social and religious changes that swept Europe, highlighting the mixed effects of the more positive valuation of marriage and family life for women. Feminist historical research has also demonstrated the significant contributions women made to nineteenth-century missionary movements, the pioneering of women's religious orders in social activism, women's involvement in anti-slavery and suffrage movements, as well as the struggle for ordination or other forms of accredited ministry.

New understandings of church

What does it mean for women to be church? A whole new feminist ecclesiology has emerged as women have reflected theologically on both their experience and their vision of church. Feminists have offered new models of church as the 'ekklesia' (Fiorenza, 1993), the roundtable or kitchen table (Russell, 1993), the household of God (Oduyoye, 2001a) and the sanctuary or place of safety (Russell, 2001). Feminists have analysed and reappraised preaching (Smith, 1989; González and González, 1994), prayer and liturgy (Proctor-Smith, 1990, 1995) and the sacraments (Ross, 1998) from the perspective of women's experiences, as well as developing broader ecclesiologies of the whole life of the church (e.g. Ruether, 1985b; Fiorenza, 1993; Russell, 1993).

Without denying the diversity of these theological analyses, various themes emerge as prominent. First, there is an emphasis on women *as* church, and a reappropriation of women's rightful gifts and authority. Women are not simply 'in' the church, as if the church pre-existed and women were simply grafted on; women constitute church and, feminists insist, constitute it in radically new ways which have not been taken seriously in the traditions of theological reflection upon the nature of church. The Womenchurch movement, and women within the churches more generally, are engaged in a revolutionary act of reappropriating what has been falsely expropriated from them. 'We are reclaiming sacramental life as the symbol of our own entry into and mutual empowerment within the redemptive life, the authentic human life or original blessing upon which we stand naturally when freed from alienating powers. Theological education and teaching are our own reflections on the meaning of reclaiming our authentic life from distortion. Ministry is the active praxis of our authentic life and the building of alternative bases of expression from which to challenge the systems of evil' (Ruether, 1985b, p. 87). Second, there is in feminist ecclesiology a prophetic critique and rejection of patriarchal and hierarchical models of church, what Ruether describes as an 'exodus from patri-archy' (1985b, p. 61) and Russell as an 'iconoclasm of patriarchy' (Russell, 1993, p. 59). Womenchurch, whether gathered as such or scattered within the institution of the church, is a denunciation of patriarchy, a 'feminist Exodus community where women delegitimise the theological myths that justify patriarchy, begin to form liturgies to midwife their liberation from it and begin to experience the gathering of liberated women as a redemptive community rooted in a new being' (Ruether, 1985b, p. 61). Third, there is a strong emphasis on church as a community of mutual ministry, where ministry is shared by all as a co-operative task of mutual empowerment. Letty Russell (1993) speaks of 'round table leadership' which should operate in communities of the Spirit, characterised by an authority in community, one focused on purpose rather than attached to particular positions or offices. 'Leadership in the round seeks to move away from the traditions of ordination and orders as authority of domination and to emphasize instead authority exercised in community. This does not deny the need for organization in the life of the church or for rituals of recognition of the gifts of the Spirit. The powers or gifts that God has given a local, regional, national or international church body need to be recognized and organized for the work of God's new household of justice and freedom' (Russell, 1993, pp. 73–74).

EXERCISE

Focus on one of the above areas – feminist practice of church, feminist church history or feminist theologies of church – to do some further reading and research. For example, make a study of feminist liturgies, read up about one specific era of church history as researched by feminist historians, or analyse one of the key theological ideas about Womenchurch proposed by feminist ecclesiologies. Review and evaluate what new insights you have gained into the nature of the church.

Further reading

Kanyoro, M R A (ed.) (1997), *In Search of a Round Table: gender, theology and church leadership*, Geneva, WCC.

McEwan, D (ed.) (1991), *Woman Experiencing Church: a documentation of alienation*, Leominster, Fowler Wright.

Parsons, S F (ed.) (2002), *The Cambridge Companion to Feminist Theology*, Cambridge, Cambridge University Press, chapter 13.

Proctor-Smith, M (1990), *In Her Own Rite: constructing feminist liturgical tradition*, Nashville, Abingdon.

Ruether, R R (1985b), *Womenchurch: theology and practice*, New York, Harper and Row.

Russell, L M (1993), *Church in the Round: feminist interpretation of the church*, Louisville, Westminster/John Knox Press.

Smith, C M (1989), *Weaving the Sermon: preaching in a feminist perspective*, Louisville, Westminster/John Knox.

St Hilda Community (1997) (2nd edition), *Women Included: a book of services and prayers*, London, SPCK.

Ward, H, Wild, J and Morley, J (eds) (1995) (2nd edition), *Celebrating Women*, London, SPCK.

Watson, N (2002), *Introducing Feminist Ecclesiology*, Sheffield, Sheffield Academic Press.

Wootton, J H (2000), *Introducing a Practical Feminist Theology of Worship*, Sheffield, Sheffield Academic Press.

9. THE HOPE FOR WHOLENESS: SPIRITUALITY IN FEMINIST PERSPECTIVE

Introduction

'Spirituality' as a term is a relatively modern one. It is also a notoriously vague and slippery concept, capable of being used in a wide variety of ways. On the one hand, the spiritual can be distinguished from the religious and understood as something wider than religiosity; on the other hand, it can be understood as the deepest and most central element of religion. It has often been understood to be concerned with interior experience, such as prayer, mystical experience and contemplation, but a broader understanding of the spiritual life as 'the life of the whole person directed towards God' [or the ultimate] (Leech, 1977, p. 34) is now more widely accepted.

In this chapter we will be focusing on patterns and understandings of spirituality as lived experience within Christianity, and how such models of holiness and the faith-filled life impacted upon women, both in the past and more recently. As in every other area of Christian life we have considered, spirituality has been an ambivalent one for women. Largely controlled by the institutional church, spirituality has been conceived and practised in body-denying, dualistic and other-worldly ways, and women's practice of spirituality has been strictly controlled by the church hierarchy. On the other hand, as Cynthia Eller (1996, p. 174) points out, 'women have consistently found, been given, or carved out a space for themselves in even the most hostile religious environments', and have developed their own religious practices and distinctive forms of spirituality down the ages. As well as critiquing androcentric and patriarchal patterns of spirituality, feminist scholarship has done much to recover women's spiritual traditions in the past, and to investigate women's contemporary spiritual practices.

> ### Reflecting on experience
> What does 'spirituality' mean to you? Do a quick brainstorm of
> the words and concepts you associate with the term, and write
> them down.
>
> What spiritual practices, if any, do you engage in?
>
> What spiritual traditions do you draw upon, and what do you
> value in them?
>
> What part have women played in your spiritual journey?
>
> Does your church or tradition honour women spiritual teachers
> and exemplars? If so, which ones, and why are they revered?

The feminist critique of spirituality

Spirituality might seem, at first sight, to be less amenable to patriarchal
abuse and control than other areas of faith; unlike the Bible, it is not
fixed and closed in the past, but a living, dynamic tradition which can
grow and change. Women have, perhaps, had greater freedom within
the spiritual realm than in other arenas of religious life. They have been
encouraged to pray, to read sacred literature, to band together with
other women and live out lives of dedicated holiness. Nevertheless,
feminists point to ways in which spirituality, like every other area of
religious life, has been controlled, shaped and dictated by men, reflecting the patriarchal bias of Christianity.

Institutional control of spirituality
Philip Sheldrake (1995) notes and demonstrates how western spirituality has been limited, controlled and defined up until recent times by
those with power in the church – essentially, celibate white male
clerics. The history of spirituality has, in reality, been the history of this
group of privileged elites within the church, and other ways of thinking
about or practising spirituality – including women's traditions and
experience – have been marginalised and suppressed. Fundamentally,
spirituality has had to conform to the needs and dictates of the institutional church and its authority structures. This is demonstrated,

Sheldrake argues, in three dominant trends which have characterised Christian spirituality.

First, 'the value of orthodoxy frequently meant the priority of majority over minority, "winners" over "losers", those who get their ideas across over the less articulate' (p. 67). The history of the church is largely a history of the 'winners', and those who in any way threatened the power base of the church hierarchy were often labelled 'heretical' and forced to comply with the centre or face excommunication, persecution and eventual extinction. Women who became too independent or exercised too much power – such as the medieval 'witches' or beguines – were curbed and controlled by the rule of orthodoxy. Second, 'conformity to the centre valued uniformity over pluralism, Establishment over new ventures, a universal culture over local experience' (p. 67). The history of Christian mission provides many chilling examples of how the church sought to stamp Eurocentric practices on indigenous cultures, wiping out local customs and ways and rendering them 'pagan' and against the way of Christ. Third, spirituality was dominated by the clerical-monastic model of holiness, and lay Christians living an ordinary family life within their local communities were expected to conform to patterns of holiness appropriate to monastic and celibate clerics. Since women were by definition lay throughout the majority of Christian history, and many were married and engaged in family life, the dominant monastic-clerical model disadvantaged them systematically.

Hierarchical and dualistic models of spirituality

In practice, then, most of the models of holiness, patterns of prayer and the literature of spirituality emanated from the experience of male celibate clerical elites, and this resulted in a dualistic hierarchy in which religious life was prized as the 'better way', celibacy was prioritised over sexual partnership and married life, priesthood was prized over the lay vocation, withdrawal from the world was favoured over active participation in it, and mysticism was vaunted over more homely patterns of prayer. Implicit in much of this theology was a fear and suspicion of the body (particularly of women's bodies) and a world-denying ethos. The flesh – especially women's flesh – and involvement in material things were associated with original sin, as we have seen in chapter 4. The body in general, then, and women in particular, had to be subdued and this led to the development of many ascetical practices and a general disengagement from matters of the material, historical and political world.

Such involvement was frequently seen as corrupting and defiling, rather than a means of serving God. Images of the Christian life as a pilgrimage or journey through an alien and hostile world to the soul's home in heaven reinforced this dualism, as did the image of 'the ladder of perfection' which the individual had to climb in order to ascend out of the fleshly, material realm, into the spiritual realm with God. In such a context, 'it was difficult to conceive of the possibility of saintliness *through* marriage or labour in the fields!' (Sheldrake, 1995, p. 70).

The hiddenness and repression of women's spirituality

Women are not the only group to be marginalised by the institutional control of spirituality from the centre, but they are the most obvious one. As Sheldrake points out, lay people in general were an 'underclass' but women in particular were denied a voice and the authority of their experience. Women, of course, practised faith, prayed and lived lives of holiness (often more devotedly than men!); and some individual women were revered for their saintliness and spiritual teaching – one thinks of Julian of Norwich, Teresa of Avila and Catherine of Sienna. Nevertheless, such women were largely exceptions to the general rule, and women's tradition of spirituality has largely been a 'hidden tradition' (Byrne, 1991). This is for a variety of complex reasons, including the clerical control and male domination of women's lives and bodies, but for other reasons too. Much women's spirituality, at least until recently, has been exercised in the home and in the care of others, particularly men and children, and thus has been expressed in the quality of life engendered by such care, but not in more overt ways. When their spirituality has taken more tangible form, it has been expressed in forms such as journals, letters, hymns, poems, needlecrafts and healing arts, rather than in systematic treatises or authoritative pronouncements, though some women in religious orders did have access to education and time which allowed them to write. For the most part, however, women's forms of expression have not been accorded public recognition, and have not been passed on as a heritage to successive generations. Even where women's spirituality did find public, institutional recognition, such as in the women's religious orders, it was usually tightly controlled by the male hierarchy. Movements such as the early Gnostic communities or the lay medieval beguine movement, in which women's spirituality flourished, were seen as dangerous by the hierarchy, and frequently pronounced heretical and/or forced to disband. When individuals such as Julian of Norwich and Teresa of Avila did achieve prominence, their stories were often seen as exceptional and therefore not to be emulated by other women, or were given a marginal place in the history of spirituality. Consider how the spiritual genius of someone like Hildegard of Bingen has been passed over in silence in most of Christian history and virtually lost to tradition until recently.

EXERCISE

Look up the lives of half a dozen saints in any dictionary of saints, making sure you choose men as well as women, and a reasonable range of historical period and place. Consider why they are regarded as 'saintly' and what values their lives enshrine.

- Are any of them married, or are they all celibate? What attitudes towards the body do their stories seem to enshrine?
- How did they relate to the wider world in which they were set? Did they demonstrate lives of active commitment to the world, or did they withdraw from the world? What do their lives demonstrate about the value of the world and its place in the pursuit of holiness?
- What spiritual practices are associated with their lives (e.g. prayer, fasting, intercession, mortification of the flesh)? What models of holiness underlie such practices?
- Did they wield power or authority? If so, of what kind? Did it receive ecclesiastical sanction? What kind of power do the women demonstrate?
- What key themes emerge from their teaching or preaching?

Try to summarise the model or models of holiness that emerge from this survey. What does it tell you about how spirituality has been practised and understood in Christian tradition?

Feminist spiritualities

Over the last three or four decades there has been an extraordinary flourishing of women's spirituality worldwide, which might itself be seen as part of a wider flowering of spiritual movements. *Feminist spirituality*, in contrast to women's spirituality more generally, arises from the consciousness of women's oppression and the commitment to overcome it. As such, it is a recent phenomenon, although it has ancient historical roots. Feminist spirituality groups and movements are multiple and diverse, existing within the mainstream churches, at their edges and way beyond the limits of church and Christianity, too.

At one end of the spectrum we find groups of women and men within the mainstream churches who are keen to recover and celebrate women's history and past spiritual traditions, and who draw on female images of God, stories of biblical women and other women-centred images and symbols in their prayer and public worship. Then there are a whole range of groups existing more on the fringes of institutional church life, often in somewhat uneasy tension with it, which seek to forge a dialogue between orthodox Christian tradition, on the one hand, and other faith traditions or secular movements, on the other, drawing on multiple sources to develop a distinctive feminist spirituality. This would include indigenous feminist movements in many parts of the world which seek to integrate Christian tradition with native sources, as well as the whole Womenchurch movement, which we considered in chapter 8, and networks such as the creation-centred spirituality movement associated with Matthew Fox and his colleagues, as well as some men's movements which seek to engage seriously with the insights of feminist theology and women's religious experience. Finally, there is a whole range of feminist groups and movements which have cut any ties with the institutional church completely, which are committed to the celebration and cultivation of women's repressed spiritual powers in female-centred traditions such as the Goddess, wicca and witchcraft traditions. These contemporary movements draw on ancient pagan symbols of the divine feminine and ancient women's wisdom, rituals and lore, as well as developing new images and practices rooted in women's bodily experience, kinship with the earth and the cycle of the seasons.

Feminist spirituality is thus a very broad-ranging movement, or more properly, a whole network of overlapping movements present in and across all the major world religions, as well as in new movements such as paganism, the Goddess movement and wicca. There are also large numbers of women with no formal allegiance to any grouping who understand their involvement in ecofeminism or justice movements as an expression of spiritual values. Whatever form it takes, feminist spirituality is concerned to recover women's neglected traditions of prayer, holiness and understandings of the spiritual life, as well as to forge new patterns of spirituality rooted in women's contemporary experience and quest for wholeness.

EXERCISE

Consider the following definitions of feminist spirituality. What are their chief emphases? What differences do you note between them? How far do you agree with them?

Feminist spirituality may be simply defined as the *praxis of imagining a whole world.* Such praxis depends on the lived experience of mutually supportive relations between self, others, God, and nature.

(Zappone, 1991, p. 13)

A specifically feminist spirituality . . . would be that mode of relating to God, and everyone and everything in relation to God, exhibited by those who are deeply aware of the historical and cultural restriction of women to a narrowly defined 'place' within the wider (male) world . . . As feminist, such a spirituality would encourage the autonomy, self-actualization, and self-transcendence of all women (and men).

(Carr, 1986, pp. 53–4)

Women's spiritual quest concerns a woman's awakening to the depths of her soul and her position in the universe . . . Women's spiritual quest involves a probing to the bedrock of a woman's experience of self and world that can support her quest to change the values of her society.

(Christ, 1986, pp. 8, 11)

Feminist spirituality 'is creation-centred rather than sin- and redemption-centred. It is holistic rather than dualistic. It is risk rather than security. It is a spirituality that is joyful rather than austere, active rather than passive, expansive rather than limiting. It celebrates more than it fasts; it lets go rather than holds back. It is an Easter rather than a Good Friday spirituality. It is vibrant, liberating, and colourful.

(Mananzan, 1994, p. 347)

Given that feminist spirituality encompasses such a wide range of diverse groups and movements, it may seem impossible to generalise about all of them, and indeed, there is a danger in trying to do so. Nevertheless, it does seem possible to identify some general trends and emphases which characterise these diverse movements and traditions.

A recovery of the body, eros and the material realm

In contrast to the dualistic, hierarchical and anti-material spiritualities which have dominated much of Christianity's history, feminist spirituality is rooted in a strong affirmation of the material realm, which includes the body and the passions, as well as the body of the earth more widely. There is a rejection of any body/spirit or earth /heaven dualism, and a celebration of the beauty and wisdom of the bodies of women (and men) and the body of the earth. This is evident in the recovery of the Goddess as a symbol of the sacredness of women's bodies, as well as in worship practices which emphasise the senses and the body as a pathway to God, and in a strong emphasis on desire, passion and eros in much contemporary feminist spirituality. Writers such as Audre Lorde (1978), Carter Heyward (1982, 1984), Rita Nakashima Brock (1988) and Mary Hunt (1991) have been influential in reclaiming the language of the erotic from the realm of the sexual, narrowly conceived, to a much wider social, political and spiritual currency. Far from fearing the body and the passions and seeking to control them, feminists trust that the body has its own instinctive wisdom which can lead to God.

The affirmation of the human body is paralleled in a strong reclamation of the earth as fundamentally good and beautiful and the locus of God; even, for some theologians, the body of God. Just as the repression and abuse of women's bodies has gone hand in hand with the rape and abuse of the earth for so many centuries, so the restoration of the goodness of women's bodies now must go hand in hand with the reclamation of the earth. For, as Elizabeth Stuart (1996, p. 24) suggests, 'The life of God's body is now at stake because of the ecological crisis: its salvation is in our hands'. Matthew Fox and feminist ecotheologians assert the need for spiritualities and theologies which are creation-centred, rather than narrowly focused on humanity and the individual's relationship with God, if the body of God is to be saved.

A strong emphasis on relationality and interconnectedness

Closely connected to the first theme, we find a strong emphasis in contemporary feminist spirituality on notions of relatedness and inter-connectedness. Spirituality is seen as fundamentally concerned with the creation of right relation – a deeply biblical notion – not only between humanity and God, but also with the self, with the human other, with the cosmos, and with God in and through all these other connections. No one thing exists in isolation but in profound and complex inter-connection with all other beings. Carter Heyward speaks of 'that fundamental relational power' which is the power of transcendence and which

> moves to cross over from people to people, race to race, gender to gender, class to class, binding us into one Body of human and created beings, healing our wounds, breaking down the assumptions and structures that keep us divided and, through it all, empowering us, each and all, to know and love ourselves and one another as participants in this transcendence. (Heyward, 1984, p. 245)

Patriarchal religion has denied that profound reality of interconnectedness through its partition and separation of things into dualist, binary opposites. Women in patriarchy have been divided and separated from each other, as well as from access to power. Feminist consciousness raising begins often with the empowering experience of sisterhood – the realisation that as a woman, I am not alone, but my sisters share my own struggles against oppression, even though our situations may be very different. Feminist spirituality seeks to reclaim the power of female connection and the empowering experience of sisterhood and female friendship. But it goes beyond interpersonal relationship to an insistence of interconnection as the warp and weft of all existence and as intrinsic to God's very being, who is known in and through right relation, wherever and however that happens.

A justice and life orientation

Justice is another way of speaking about right relation. There can be no right relation between persons, groups or societies without justice, or at least a strong commitment to working towards justice. With other liberation movements, feminist spiritualities exhibit a strong commitment to justice and the redemption of political and structural relationships, not simply the redemption of the individual. If all things are connected, there can be no simplistic division between the private and the public, the personal and the political. There is no spiritual liberation which is not also political freedom, there is no salvation which is not manifested in a greater abundance of life, in real material terms. In contrast to much traditional piety, which has been concerned with the

destiny of the individual soul beyond death, feminist spirituality has a
strong life orientation, and is deeply concerned with the maintenance
and sustenance of life in all its fullness here and now. Some see this life-
orientation as rooted in women's biological capacity to give birth and in
their ancient role as the nurturers of life; as Luz Beatriz Arellano (1994,
p. 321) suggests, 'Being essentially bearers and sustainers of life, women
find a new meaning in the discovery of God as God of life, and they
themselves become stronger and more conscious as defenders and
bearers of life, not only in the biological sense but in all its dimensions.'

Whether or not it is biologically shaped, this life orientation cannot
be separated from the struggle for justice, for life is threatened in many
parts of the globe and in many contexts by injustice, ecological crisis
and systems of oppression. This commitment to the preservation and
sustenance of life within the pursuit of justice is particularly evident in
the spiritualities of so-called 'third-world' feminists, where the inter-
connection between spiritual well-being and socio-political liberation is
glaringly obvious.

An insistence on holism, inclusivity and integration

It is obvious from all that has gone before that a feminist spirituality is
a strongly holistic and inclusive spirituality that rejects any and every
dualism, whether of mind and body, God and world or personal and
political. Holiness is understood within feminist spiritualities largely in
terms of wholeness of life, and the aim of spirituality is integration of
all life in the one vision of justice and freedom for all. As Anne Carr
(1986, p. 49) puts it, 'spirituality is holistic, encompassing our relationships to all of creation – to others, to society and nature, to work and
recreation – in a fundamentally religious orientation'. This commitment
to holism and integration also manifests itself in an inclusive stance
within feminist spiritualities, an openness to recognise the movement of
the Spirit in all justice, peace and liberation movements and in all
people of goodwill, whatever their religious commitment or lack of it.
Truth is known by its fruits, rather than its academic or religious pedi-
gree, and the real test of God at work and the Spirit's presence is the
fruits of justice, freedom, love, compassion, solidarity with the
oppressed and care of the earth. The Spirit is at work wherever human
beings are working towards the freedom and liberation of the earth and
its creatures, whether such work is motivated consciously by religious
impulses or not.

EXERCISE

Write a manifesto of feminist spirituality, using a repeated refrain such as 'Spirituality is . . .' or 'To be a spiritual person means . . .' or 'Holiness consists in . . .'. Compare your version with Mary's Magnificat in Luke 1:46–56 and with Phoebe Willetts' paraphrase (in Ward, Wild and Morley, 1995, p. 37):

My heart is bubbling over with joy:
with God it is good to be woman.
From now on let all peoples proclaim:
it is a wonderful gift to be.
The one in whom power truly rests
has lifted us up to praise;
God's goodness shall fall like a shower
on the trusting of every age.
The disregarded have been raised up:
the pompous and powerful shall fall.
God has feasted the empty-bellied,
and the rich have discovered their void.
God has made good the word
given at the dawn of time.

Further reading

Byrne, L (1991), *The Hidden Tradition: women's spiritual writings rediscovered*, London, SPCK.

Carr, A (1986), On feminist spirituality, in J W Conn (ed.), *Women's Spirituality: resources for Christian development*, New York, Paulist Press, pp. 49–58.

King, U (1989), *Women and Spirituality: voices of protest and promise*, Basingstoke, Macmillan.

King, U (ed.) (1994), *Feminist Theology from the Third World: a reader*, London, SPCK, Part five.

Sheldrake, P (1995) (2nd edition), *Spirituality and History: questions of interpretation and method*, London, SPCK.

Slee, N (2002) The Holy Spirit and spirituality, in S F Parsons (ed.), *The Cambridge Companion to Feminist Theology*, Cambridge, Cambridge University Press, pp.171–189.

Zappone, K (1991), *The Hope for Wholeness: a spirituality for feminists*, Mystic, Conn., Twenty-Third Publications.

10. THE FUTURE OF FEMINIST THEOLOGY: GIFT AND CHALLENGE TO THE CHURCHES

Introduction

Feminism undoubtedly represents one of the most significant challenges to traditional patriarchal patterns of thinking and forms of life, including the self-consciousness and social organisation of religion. Specifically, the feminist critique of Christianity represents perhaps the most radical and far-reaching contemporary challenge to the self-understanding and future of the church. Yet, at the same time, feminism represents the possibility of transformation and renewal of religious faith in our time, if the churches can be courageous enough to submit themselves to its critique and engage in serious dialogue with its representatives. This chapter emphasises the enormous creativity and life-giving potential of feminist theology and affirms it as gift, as well as challenge, to the churches.

And yet it would be misleading to make it sound as if the challenge were one way only: feminism may well represent one of the most radical challenges to Christian self-understanding, but, at the same time, feminism itself is under threat and challenge from many different quarters in the contemporary scene. The feminism of the seventies and eighties has undergone huge shifts as a result of complex social, political and intellectual influences, and just about every confident claim of the early second-wave feminists is now contested. Some suggest we inhabit a 'post-feminist' era in which the claims and demands of feminism have either been met or have been shown to be illusory. Whether this is so or not, it is certainly the case that the changing face of secular feminism is beginning to have an impact on feminist theology in profound ways, and feminist theology itself is undergoing major rethinking and reorientation. And if developments in the wider, secular world have something to say to feminist theology, so, too, does Christian faith. Feminist theology has at times, perhaps, been too uncritical in taking on board the assumptions, presuppositions and values of secular feminism without submitting them to radical challenge. One of the gifts of Christian faith to feminist theology is its provision of a radically alternative world-view: and, though feminists have wanted to critique and challenge that world-view in many ways, there may still be Christian insights and values which have something to say to feminism itself.

In this chapter, then, we consider the ways in which feminist theology itself is changing and facing challenge, as well as the ways in which Christianity is challenged to change by feminist theology. This is inevitably a provisional appraisal, for, even as I write, the situation is changing, and by the time this is published, the situation will have moved on again.

Reflecting on experience

Stop and reflect back on your experience of reading this book and undertaking a study of feminist theology.
- What key insights have you gained?
- What have you found exciting, liberating or affirming?
- What have you found challenging, difficult or threatening?
- How do you view Christian faith now in the light of your study?

The changing face of feminist theology

Where does feminist theology stand now? What is its place within academia and within the churches? Three or four decades on from the pioneering work of second-wave feminists in the sixties and seventies, feminist theology has changed in many complex and subtle ways, some of which we take note of below.

The massive proliferation, diversity and fragmentation of feminist theology

As we have noted repeatedly throughout this book, feminist theology has diversified and proliferated in many different forms as it has developed, taking root and finding expression in countless different cultural settings. Feminist theology is breaking out of the confines of its earlier, predominantly white, middle-class box. Some of the most exciting and original work is now being done by feminist theologians in

Africa, Asia and South America. The cultural diversity of womanist, mujerista, minjung and dalit perspectives is joined by lesbian and queer theology (e.g. Althaus-Reid, 2001), feminist theologies of disability (e.g. Freeman, 2002) and perspectives which bring together diverse locations, operating across multiple lines of identity and oppression. For example, in a recent issue of *Feminist Theology*, Laura Donaldson (2002) writes out of what she calls the 'contact zone' where indigenous American Indian traditions encountered colonial Christianity, whilst Jean Zaru (2002) analyses the oppression she experiences at the juncture of multiple intersecting identities: as Palestinian, as Christian, as Quaker, as woman. It is not possible to categorise such theologies in simple, neat terms. Just as gender theory has challenged any simplistic, essentialist reading of gender, so we need to abandon essentialist notions of race, culture, class, sexual identity and disability. To label any theology 'womanist' or 'queer' or 'disabled' can only operate as a convenient shorthand, but cannot divulge the characteristics, qualities or concerns of that theology. We can only listen to the distinct voice of each person speaking to hear what it is they have to say. And, with every day, we are aware of more and more voices speaking. 'The once single voice has fragmented into a cacophany', as Sawyer and Collier (1999, p. 11) put it. This growing diversification of feminist theology is ambivalent. It is both an immeasurable enrichment of feminist theology and, at the same time, a potential fragmentation of the clear, single voice that spoke out in the early days of feminist critique and demand. The challenge facing feminist theology is, in the words of Pamela Dickey Young (1995, p. 76), to 'privilege diversity without fragmenting into "communities" of one'.

The increasing academic sophistication, rigour and specialisation of feminist theology

Although there are major differences between different cultural contexts, and there are places where feminist theology remains excluded from the academy (for example, in Germany, where the German universities remain closely linked to the churches and the church hierarchy has maintained control over academic appointments, few feminist theologians have found academic posts), nevertheless, feminist theology certainly has become quite firmly established within the universities in many countries, particularly in Northern America and many European countries. There are now many opportunities for women to study feminist theology at undergraduate and postgraduate level, and the proliferation of literature, journals and societies connected with feminist theology is testimony to the health and vitality of feminist theology as an academic discipline. Or rather, we should say, academic disciplines in the plural, for, as feminist theology has developed, it has become increasingly sophisticated and specialised. Every area of feminist theology – biblical studies, church history, doctrine, ethics, practical theology, philosophy of religion and so on – has its own specialised terminology, methods and literature. It is now quite impossible to keep abreast of all the developments in any one of these sub-disciplines, let alone to be competent across all of them. This increasing sophistication and academic respectability of feminist theology is, perhaps, an ambivalent achievement. On the one hand, it gives feminist theology greater credibility and footing in the academic world than it has had previously, and makes it less likely that it can simply be ignored and sidelined by other academics (although there is enough evidence of the marginal position of feminist theology within academic faculties to keep one from being sanguine). On the other hand, as feminist theology becomes increasingly located in the academic world, there is a real danger that it loses its connection with grass-roots groups and communities of women, and with the political struggle for justice, and that it becomes increasingly alienated from the everyday concerns and lives of ordinary women. As Dorothea McEwan (1999, p. 82) suggests, 'The academic speculative stance of feminist theologies . . . will be but a glass bead game of no consequence, of no future . . . if it is not bounced against practice, most notably the church's/es' relationship to women'.

The shift from feminism to a broader gender perspective

A major theoretical shift has taken place in feminism generally in the late eighties and nineties and, consequently, in feminist theology. This is the shift from a feminist perspective focused on the liberation of women from gender oppression and the commitment to doing theology from the bias of women's experience, to a broader and more critically aligned gender perspective. This shift has come about partly through the critical work of secular theorists who have challenged the early, somewhat simplistic notions of gender which feminists held, and partly through the development of men's studies and the deconstruction of gender from other perspectives than a female one. Whereas, in the 1960s, 70s and even the 80s, gender was assumed to refer to a relatively stable category such that women were supposed to be in a certain way and men in another, this 'gender essentialism' has increasingly come under fire, and from a number of quarters. First, as feminists became increasingly conscious of diversity amongst women, so it began to be acknowledged that women construct gender in many different ways: it is impossible to make global claims about 'women's experience'. So, too, men's studies have begun to demonstrate how differently different men construct masculinity. More broadly, theorists such as Judith Butler (1990) have challenged the very notion of gender as something fixed and related in straightforward ways to sex. Butler's notions of gender as performance and sex as a cultural construction are intriguing and difficult, and too complex to attempt to summarise here, but at the very least they invite us to think about gender and sex in much more fluid ways than previously.

What this means for feminist theory in general, and feminist theology in particular, is by no means straightforward. On the one hand, the move to a broader gender perspective is positive in that it has the capacity to be much more inclusive than feminism has previously been – of men as well as women, of diverse cultural constructions of gender, of different sexual identities, and so on – and thereby to insist that how gender is constructed and experienced, and how this relates to faith, is an issue for all, and not simply for women. As Ursula King (1995, p. 8) suggests, 'the strength of a critical, but more inclusive gender studies lies in its greater comprehensiveness through seeing femaleness and maleness, and the attendant constructions of masculinity and femininity, as closely interrelated'. On the other hand, the breaking down of the earlier construct of 'women' threatens the viability of feminism and feminist theology for, as Iris Young suggests, 'without some sense in which "woman" is the name of a social collective, there is nothing specific to feminist politics' (1994, p. 714). The broader focus on gender can lead to the dissipation of feminism's early insistence on the oppression of women and the struggle for liberation.

The critique of feminist theology from within

As feminist theology has matured and diversified, so the voices of critical appraisal and debate have multiplied. Whilst feminist theology has always been criticised from without, sometimes quite viciously, here I am thinking of the rise of positive and informed critical debate from *within*. In the early days, when feminists were largely concerned with deconstructing centuries of oppressive patriarchal religion, and when each feminist scholar of religion was very often a lone voice in her own particular field, there was little possibility of internal critical debate and not much stomach for it. That has now changed. As Ursula King (1999, p. 101) asserts, 'feminist theology's own critical claims must themselves come under critical examination, and there is now sufficient material of enough substance and variety to do this in a spirit of openness and critical reflexivity'. As feminist theology has become more established within academia and within general theological discourse, and as the diversity of feminist theological perspectives has multiplied, so the possibility of internal critical debate has intensified. This is demonstrated in collections such as *Swallowing a Fishbone*, edited by Daphne Hampson (1996), in which Christian feminist theologians engaged in robust dialogue with Hampson, a post-Christian, about the possibilities of being both Christian and feminist; and the anthology of essays entitled, *Is There a Future for Feminist Theology?*, edited by Deborah Sawyer and Diane Collier (1999), in which a wide variety of scholars, both women and men, considered the state and future of feminist theology; as well as by the ongoing debate in journals such as *Feminist Theology* and the *Journal of Feminist Studies of Religion*. Robust dialogue and critical scrutiny across difference have become the norm, not the exception. Whereas critics from outside may have lambasted feminist theology for being unbiblical, heretical and unorthodox, driven by secularism and an 'unChristian' desire for power (e.g. Oddie, 1984), the critique from within has been more intelligent, more nuanced and more constructive – but none the less compelling, for all that. Feminists have critiqued feminist theology for a tendency to reinscribe those very evils it abhors in patriarchal theology: for a universalising and totalising perspective which ignores difference, particularly racial and cultural difference (e.g. Grant, 1989; Thislethwaite, 1990; Williams, 1993); for operating with simplistic binary oppositions that polarise (e.g. King, 1999); and for operating in a separatist ghetto, isolated from other disciplines and theological perspectives which belies its rhetoric of relationality (King, 1999; Woodhead, 1999). Others have critiqued feminist Christians for adopting an infantile 'victim' status which insists on women's innocence and does not take responsibility for women's complicity in structures of evil (West, 1995); or for preaching an implicit theology of 'salvation through women' which simply reverses the patriarchal idolisation of masculinity and refuses the universality of salvation (Alresford, 1999).

> **EXERCISE**
> Consider the changes in recent feminist theology identified above.
> • How significant do you rate each of them?
> • Do you see them as 'good' or 'bad' or both? Why?
> • What difference do you see such changes making to feminist theology?

The future of feminist theology

What, then, of the future of feminist theology? Does it have a future and, if so, what shape and focus will that future take? The estimation of commentators and critics varies widely. Some are hopeful, and see the current developments in feminist theology as indications of its vitality and strength, signs that it has limitless potential to change and grow and adapt to meet the needs of new situations and understandings. Others consider that feminist theology remains too ghettoised, too little in dialogue with secular gender theory or with other theological views and perspectives, and is thus in danger of atrophying and being ignored by the wider theological establishment. Others again consider that feminist theology has run its course; by raising the awareness of women's oppression and marginalisation and by reclaiming women's history and rewriting theology from women's perspective, it has largely achieved its ends and can be absorbed into a new, broader, more inclusive theology.

> **EXERCISE**
> Consider the quotations below and organise a discussion with others on the future of feminist theology.
>
> Feminist theology now stands at a cross-roads, faced with choices of the most far-reaching consequence for its future shape . . . The most significant of these choices concerns feminist theology's willingness to move more decisively into dialogue with the Christian tradition, with other disciplines and audiences, and to free itself from an isolation that threatens its future. (Woodhead, 1999, p. 198)
>
>

We have created, are continuing to create, a new theological paradigm. New theological paradigms are about as rare as new scientific paradigms, yet, unbelievably, it has happened, it is happening now, and we are the epistemic community that is doing it. I find it so exciting to be a feminist theologian that sometimes I have to jump up and down. (Tatman, 2002, p. 46)

In the next decade or so there will be another generation of women singing a new song, and no doubt also another generation of women theological scholars who, we may hope and expect, will further strengthen the new and exciting field of feminist theologies through creative, critical and lively debates that will not only affect and transform women's experience and reflections, but also make a lasting mark on the future shape of theology itself. (King, 1999, pp. 113–114)

Initially, perhaps the development of feminist theology necessitated an uncritical engagement with the resources of secular feminism, but the time has come to develop a more critical spirit of discernment. (Beattie, 1999, p. 125)

The ultimate aim of feminist theology is to work towards its own demise as a distinct discipline. The final desirable state of affairs is one in which there is no need of feminist theology because its insights and emphases have been incorporated into the way theology is done . . . (Page, 1999, p. 193)

The challenge to Christianity

If feminist theologies themselves are in a process of flux and change, and their future is uncertain, the same may be said of Christian faith and practice. This is nothing new in itself. Christianity has always been growing and changing, adapting to new situations, contexts and times – not always, of course, with sensitivity to the locations in which it found itself, but often imposing alien cultural norms as it travelled or retreating from cultural challenges. And if feminist theology is multiple and varied, so, too is Christian tradition. There has never been and never will be only one form or expression of Christian belief: as a world faith, Christianity is as multiform, diverse, complex and fluid as any other historical tradition which has survived for millennia in vastly different contexts. Nevertheless, Christianity, along with every other world faith, faces contemporary challenges which are qualitatively new in comparison with anything these traditions have previously faced. The diverse faces of feminism throughout the world are part of this new, qualitative challenge – not the only part, but a highly significant part all the same.

What impact is feminism having upon the changing shape of Christian life and faith? How is and will the church respond to this uprising of women's power and voice? It is probably too soon to say. Whilst the outcome remains uncertain, there are a number of points that can be made about the nature of the challenge facing Christianity.

Feminist theology focuses and sharpens the critique on religion of post-modernity

Feminists are not the only ones who are disenchanted with institutional religion. In the melée of post-modernity, when grand narrative, traditional truths, universal systems and public institutions of all kind have come under attack, the church is only one of the more obvious institutions to be facing a severe crisis of identity, and to be facing it from many quarters. Government, the legal system, policing and educational institutions all face similar challenge and critique. In its assault on traditional, patriarchal religion, feminist theology can be understood as one strand of this larger, post-modern critique, in which all of the achievements of modernity – rationality, the notion of the independent subject, the equality of free males, democracy, and so on – are being deconstructed and shown to be the partial achievements they were, privileging white, educated, European men of power, but leaving out vast tracts of humanity from consideration, of whom women were one, and perhaps the largest constituency, but not the only one. Feminist theology simply focuses and sharpens this wider post-modern critique on religion from the perspective of this particular constituency, women. It shares much in common with other discourses of disenfranchised groups and needs to be in dialogue and co-operation with black theology, queer theology, body theology, urban theology, and other forms of liberation theology. Women's liberation cannot and will not be achieved in isolation from the liberation of all who find themselves marginalised from the Enlightenment project of liberty, equality and fraternity. But if feminism is part of this larger post-modern critique, it also needs to beware of taking on too blithely the presuppositions of post-modernity. As many feminists have pointed out, women should not be too hasty to join the post-modern project of dismantling the rational, autonomous, modern self, when women as a collective are only just coming into their own selfhood and working out what female subjectivity might mean. Feminism may share some of the goals of postmodernity, but it may want to reject others.

Feminism's critique of Christianity is fundamental, not superficial

Despite the efforts of some of its critics to trivialise and dismiss feminist theology, it is clear that the feminist critique of religion strikes to the heart of religious truth and identity. This, at least, the conservative elements within the church have recognised; when they castigate and demonise the feminist cause, they acknowledge its power and its significance. As we have seen throughout this book, feminist theology raises profound questions about every aspect of Christian faith and life. The nature and names of God, the authority and authenticity of the scriptures, the significance and meaning of Christ, the nature and extent of redemption, the inclusivity of the church – these, and many more fundamentals of Christian faith, have come under the severest attack. The challenge is not superficial, but fundamental, raising profound questions about the self-identity of Christianity. As Daly puts it, 'The entire conceptual systems of theology and ethics, developed under the conditions of patriarchy, have been the products of males and tend to serve the interests of sexist society . . . The women's critique is not of a few passages but of a universe of sexist suppositions' (1986, pp. 4, 5). The challenge raised by feminist theologies will not be met by superficial change, by mere tinkering with the surface of things. Simply naming God 'mother' as well as 'father', admitting women into the clerical camp by ordaining them, imaging Christ as a woman, even a queer one, stretching the boundaries of ecclesiastical practice a little; none of this will do. The response of the tradition must be far more serious, far more radical, if Christianity is to survive into the future as more than a fossilised, decaying religion.

At the same time, it is important to say that the challenge and critique is not only one-way. Feminism certainly has hard things to say to

Christian tradition (as well as life-giving gifts to offer), but so, too, does Christian tradition have things to say to feminism. As Tina Beattie (1999) has suggested, if Christianity uncritically conforms itself to secular discourses, including feminism, it risks losing its identity and becoming the 'poor relation' of secular theory. An incarnational Christian faith has its own distinctive truths and challenges to bring to the dialogue between faith and feminism, demanding 'a recognition of the crucifying power of this world, the treachery of the social order, and the ultimately fickle allegiances of populist movements, even those that are politically correct' (p. 125). Christian faith must make seismic changes in response to the demands and gifts of feminism, but it must also bear witness faithfully to the subversive gospel of Jesus Christ, the incarnational nature of God's involvement in the world, the communitarian nature of divinity who is power in mutual relation – and many of these truths are profoundly counter-cultural.

Christianity contains the potential to respond creatively to the feminist challenge

Can Christianity respond creatively to the challenges and the gifts of women around the world who are no longer content to put up with reality as it is, but who are demanding and offering a new vision of faith and praxis? This remains a question which divides both feminists and Christian commentators more widely. I have argued elsewhere that 'Christian tradition is indeed capable of the kind of transformation which feminism requires of it' (1996, p. 34), since Christian tradition is, itself, a dynamic, fluid cluster of lived stories which, rightly understood, have always been open to change, even radical, subversive change. I do not understand Christianity to be a set of fixed blueprints, either ideological or behavioural, which have been set down once-for-all in the past and which subsequent generations of believers live out more or less faithfully. 'A Christian', I have suggested, 'is one who lives in creative, fruitful relation to the Jesus-story, rather than one who believes certain doctrines about Jesus as the Christ . . . the defining characteristic of the Christian is the lived relation to the story, rather than a particular set of beliefs about the story' (1996, p. 37). This is not to say that beliefs do not matter, but it is to recognise that theological reflection and articulation is 'second act' that comes after the 'first act' of lived faith. It is also to recognise that diverse, even conflicting, theological interpretations of the Jesus story have always been a part of Christian faith, and always will be.

EXERCISE

Consider the following different views on Christianity's capacity to respond to the challenges and gifts of feminist theology. With which do you agree most, and why?

Why anyone who calls herself (or himself) a feminist, who believes in human equality, should wish to hold to a patriarchal myth such as Christianity must remain a matter for bafflement. (Hampson, 1996, p. 50)

Is it possible to be a Christian and a feminist at the same time, and if so, how? In answer to this question, I wish to say 'Yes, but only if Christian identity is understood in a sufficiently flexible and dynamic way; only if Christian identity is understood to be open to continual renewal, reformation and transformation; and only if feminism itself is permitted to become an agent of Christianity's own transformation.' (Slee, 1996, p. 33)

It seems to me inappropriate and misleading to consider feminism the deathknell of Christianity, for although the institutional structures may be changed beyond recognition, there is no doubt that Christianity still possesses great reservoirs of hope and large scriptural, historical and spiritual resources for empowering women to seek liberation and justice. (King, 1999, p. 113)

Sexism has had its day and Christian theology, that has perpetuated it with its history of 'neuroses' regarding human sexuality, has a responsibility to play a more positive role. Religion has what it takes to do this. (Oduyoye, 2001b, p. 120)

Further reading

Fiorenza, E Schüssler and Shawn Copeland, M (eds.) (1996), *Feminist Theology in Different Contexts (Concilium 1995 and 1996)*, London, SCM.

Hampson, D (ed.) (1996), *Swallowing a Fishbone: feminist theologians debate Christianity*, London, SPCK.

Kyung, C H (1990), *Struggle To Be The Sun Again: introducing Asian women's theology*, London, SCM, chapter 7.

Loades, A (1999), Mission, inculturation and the liberation of genders: the contribution of feminist theology, *Feminist Theology*, 20, 87–98.

Oduyoye, M A (2001), *Introducing African Women's Theology*, Sheffield, Sheffield Academic Press, chapter 9.

Sawyer, D F and Collier, D M (eds) (1999), *Is There a Future for Feminist Theology?*, Sheffield, Sheffield Academic Press.

Slee, N. (1996), The power to re-member, in D Hampson (ed.), *Swallowing a Fishbone: feminist theologians debate Christianity*, London, SPCK, pp. 33–49.

Tatman, L (1999), Thoughts and hopes on the future of feminist theology/ies, *Feminist Theology*, 22, 93–100.

REFERENCES

Alsford, S (1999), Women's nature and the feminization of theology, in D F Sawyer and D M Collier (eds), *Is There a Future for Feminist Theology?*, Sheffield, Sheffield Academic Press, pp. 126–138.

Althaus-Reid, M (1999), On wearing skirts without underwear, *Feminist Theology*, 20, 39–51.

Althaus-Reid, M (2001), *Indecent Theology: theological perversions in sex, gender and politics*, London, Routledge.

Arellano, L B (1994), Women's experience of God in emerging spirituality, in U King (ed.), *Feminist Theology from the Third World: a reader*, London, SPCK, pp. 318–338.

Atkinson, C (1991), *The Oldest Vocation: Christian motherhood in the Middle Ages*, New York, Cornell University Press.

Beattie, T (1999), Global sisterhood or wicked stepsisters: why don't girls with god-mothers get invited to the ball?, in D F Sawyer and D M Collier (eds), *Is There a Future for Feminist Theology?*, Sheffield, Sheffield Academic Press, pp. 115–126.

Boff, L (1987), *The Maternal Face of God: the feminine and its religious expressions*, Maryknoll, Orbis.

Brock, R N (1988), *Journeys By Heart: a christology of erotic power*, New York, Crossroad.

Brock, R N (1989), And a little child will lead us: Christology and child abuse, in J C Brown and C R Bohn (eds), *Christianity, Patriarchy, and Abuse: a feminist critique*, New York, Pilgrim Press, pp. 42–61.

Brown, J C and Bohn, C R (eds) (1989), *Christianity, Patriarchy, and Abuse: a feminist critique*, New York, Pilgrim Press.

Brown, J C and Parker, J (1989), For God so loved the world?, in J C Brown and C R Bohn (eds), *Christianity, Patriarchy, and Abuse: a feminist critique*, New York, Pilgrim Press, pp. 1–30.

Butler, J (1990), *Gender Trouble: feminism and the subversion of identity*, New York, Routledge.

Bynum, C W (1982), *Jesus as Mother*, Berkeley, University of California Press.

Bynum, C W (1987), *Holy Feast and Holy Fast: the religious significance of food to medieval women*, Berkeley, University of California Press.

Byrne, L (1991), *The Hidden Tradition: women's spiritual writings rediscovered*, London, SPCK.

Carr, A (1986), On feminist spirituality, in J W Conn (ed.), *Women's Spirituality: resources for Christian development*, New York, Paulist Press, pp. 49–58.

Christ, C (1986) (2nd edition), *Diving Deep and Surfacing: women writers on spiritual quest*, Boston, Beacon Press.

Christ, C (2002), Feminist theology as post-traditional theology, in S F Parsons (ed.), *The Cambridge Companion to Feminist Theology*, Cambridge, Cambridge University Press, pp. 79–96.

Clanton, J Aldridge (1991), *In Whose Image? God and gender*, London, SCM.

Clark, E (1986), *Ascetic Piety and Women's Faith: essays on late ancient Christianity*, Lewiston, NY, Edwin Mellen Press.

Congar, Y (1983), *I Believe in the Holy Spirit*, 3 volumes, New York, Seabury.

Crawford, J (1996), Church history, in L Isherwood and D McEwan (eds), *An A to Z of Feminist Theology*, Sheffield, Sheffield Academic Press, pp. 27–30.

Daly, M (1986) (2nd edition), *Beyond God the Father: towards a philosophy of women's liberation*, London, Women's Press.

Dietrich, G (2001), *A New Thing on Earth: hopes and fears facing feminist theology*, Delhi, ISPCK.

Donaldson, L E (2002), Native women's double cross: Christology from the contact zone, *Feminist Theology*, 29, 96–117.

Douglas, K B (1994), *The Black Christ*, Maryknoll, Orbis.

Douglas, K B (1996), Christ, Jesus, in L M Russell and J S Clarkson (eds), *Dictionary of Feminist Theologies*, London, Mowbray, pp. 38–39.

Dowell, S and Hurcombe, L (1981), *Dispossessed Daughters of Eve: faith and feminism*, London, SCM.

Dunfee, S N (1982), The sin of hiding, *Soundings*, 65, 25–35.

Eisland, N (1994), *The Disabled God: Toward a Liberatory Theology of Disability*, Nashville, Abingdon.

Eller, C (1996), Spirituality, Women's, in L M Russell and J S Clarkson (eds), *Dictionary of Feminist Theologies*, London, Mowbray, pp. 274–277.

Fabella, V and Parks, S A L (1989), *We Dare to Dream: doing theology as Asian women*, Maryknoll, Orbis.

Fiorenza, E Schüssler (1983), *In Memory of Her: a feminist theological reconstruction of Christian origins*, London, SCM.

Fiorenza, E Schüssler (1984), *Bread Not Stone: the challenge of feminist biblical interpretation*, Boston, Beacon.

Fiorenza, E Schüssler (1993), *Discipleship of Equals: a critical feminist ecclesiology of liberation*, New York, Crossroad.

Fiorenza, E Schüssler (1995), *Jesus: Miriam's child, Sophia's prophet*, London, SCM.

Fox, M. (1983), *Original Blessing: a primer in creation spirituality*, Sante Fe, Bear and Co.

Fox, M (1991), *Creation Spirituality: liberating gifts for the peoples of the earth*, San Francisco, HarperSanFrancisco.

Freeman, D (2002), A feminist theology of disability, *Feminist Theology*, 29, 71–85.

Gelpi, D (1984), *The Divine Mother: a trinitarian theology of the Holy Spirit*, Lanham, University Press of America.

González, J L and González, C G (1994), *The Liberating Pulpit*, Nashville, Abingdon.

Grant, J (1989), *White Women's Christ and Black Women's Jesus: feminist christology and womanist response*, Atlanta, Scholars Press.

Grey, M (1989), *Redeeming the Dream: feminism, redemption and Christian tradition*, London, SPCK.

Hampson, D (1990), *Theology and Feminism*, Oxford, Blackwell.

Hampson, D (ed.) (1996), *Swallowing a Fishbone: feminist theologians debate Christianity*, London, SPCK.

Hampson, D (1996), *After Christianity*, London, SCM.

Harding, S (1986), *The Science Question in Feminism*, Milton Keynes, Open University Press.

Heyward, C (1982), *The Redemption of God: a theology of mutual relation*, Washington, DC, University Press of America.

Heyward, C (1984), *Our Passion for Justice*, New York, Pilgrim Press.

Heyward, C (1989), *Touching Our Strength: the erotic as power and the love of God*, San Francisco, Harper and Row.

Heyward, C (1999), *Saving Jesus From Those Who Are Right*, Minneapolis, Fortress.

Hogan, L (1995), *From Women's Experience to Feminist Theology*, Sheffield, Sheffield Academic Press.

Hunt, M (1991), *Fierce Tenderness: a feminist theology of friendship*, New York, Crossroad.

Hunt, M (1996), Women-Church, in L Isherwood and D McEwan (eds), *An A to Z of Feminist Theology*, Sheffield, Sheffield Academic Press, pp. 240–241.

Johnson, E (1992), *She Who Is: the mystery of God in feminist theological discourse*, New York, Crossroad.

Kim, G Ji-Sun (2001), Revisioning Christ, *Feminist Theology*, 28, 82–92.

King, U (1989), *Women and Spirituality: voices of protest and promise*, Basingstoke, Macmillan.

King, U (ed.) (1994), *Feminist Theology from the Third World: a reader*, London, SPCK.

King, U (ed.) (1995), *Religion and Gender*, Oxford, Blackwell.

King, U (1999), Feminist theologies in contemporary contexts: a provisional assessment, in D F Sawyer and D M Collier (eds), *Is There a Future for Feminist Theology?*, Sheffield, Sheffield Academic Press, pp. 100–114.

Kyung, C H (1991), *Struggle To Be The Sun Again*, London, SCM.

Leech, K (1977), *Soul Friend,* London, Darton, Longman and Todd.

Lorde, A (1978), *Uses of the Erotic: the erotic as power*, Freedom, CA, The Crossing Point.

Maitland, S (1983), *A Map of the New Country: women and Christianity*, London, Routledge and Kegan Paul.

Mananzan, M J (1994), Theological perspectives of a religious woman today – four trends of the emerging spirituality, in U King (ed.), *Feminist Theology from the Third World: a reader*, London, SPCK, pp. 340–349.

Marriage, A (1989), *Life-Giving Spirit: responding to the feminine in God*, London, SPCK.

McEwan, D (1999), The future of Christian feminist theologies – as I sense it, *Feminist Theology*, 22, 79–92.

McFague, S (1987), *Models of God: theology for an ecological, nuclear age*, London, SCM.

McFague, S (1993), *The Body of God: an ecological theology*, London, SCM.

Miles, M R (1992), *Carnal Knowing: female nakedness and religious meaning in the Christian west*, Tunbridge Wells, Burns and Oates.

Moltmann, J (1981), *The Trinity and the Kingdom of God*, London, SCM.

Morley, J (1984), 'The faltering words of men': exclusive language in the liturgy, in M Furlong (ed.), *Feminine in the Church*, London, SPCK, pp. 56–70.

Ochschorn, J (1981), *The Female Experience and the Nature of the Divine*, Bloomington, Indiana University Press.

Oddie, W (1984), *What Will Happen to God?* London, SPCK.

Oduyoye, M (2001a), A biblical perspective on the Church, *Ecumenical Review*, 53, 44–47.

Oduyoye, M (2001b), *Introducing African Women's Theology*, Sheffield, Sheffield Academic Press.

Page, R (1999), Has feminist theology a viable long-term future?, in D F Sawyer and D M Collier (eds), *Is There a Future for Feminist Theology*, Sheffield, Sheffield Academic Press, pp. 193–197.

Parsons, S Frank (2002), *The Cambridge Companion to Feminist Theology*, Cambridge, Cambridge University Press.

Phillips, J A (1984), *Eve: the history of an idea*, San Francisco, Harper and Row.

Plaskow, J (1980), *Sex, Sin and Grace: women's experience in the theologies of Reinhold Niebuhr and Paul Tillich*, Lanham, University Press of America.

Primavesi, A (1991), *From Apocalypse to Genesis: ecology, feminism and Christianity*, London, Burns and Oates.

Proctor-Smith, M (1990), *In Her Own Rite: constructing feminist liturgical tradition*, Nashville, Abingdon.

Proctor-Smith, M (1995), *Praying With Our Eyes Open: engendering feminist liturgical prayer*, Nashville, Abingdon.

Pui-Lan, K (2002), Feminist theology as intercultural discourse, in S F Parsons (ed.), *The Cambridge Companion to Feminist Theology*, Cambridge, Cambridge University Press, pp. 23–39.

Ross, S A (1998), *Extravagant Affections: a feminist sacramental theology*, New York, Continuum.

Ross, S A (2002), Church and sacrament – community and worship, in S F Parsons (ed.), *The Cambridge Companion to Feminist Theology*, Cambridge, Cambridge University Press, pp. 224–242.

Ruether, R Radford (1983), *Sexism and God-Talk*, London, SCM.

Ruether, R Radford (1985a), *Womanguides: readings toward a feminist theology*, Boston, Beacon Press.

Ruether, R Radford (1985b), *Women-Church: theology and practice of feminist liturgical communities*, New York, Harper and Row.

Ruether, R Radford (1998), *Introducing Redemption in Christian Feminism*, Sheffield, Sheffield Academic Press.

Russell, L M (1993), *Church in the Round: feminist interpretation of the church*, Louisville, Westminster/John Knox Press.

Russell, L (2001), Hot-house ecclesiology: a feminist interpretation of the church, *Ecumenical Review*, 53, 48–56.

Sawyer, D F and Collier, D M (eds) (1999), *Is There a Future for Feminist Theology?*, Sheffield, Sheffield Academic Press.

Sheldrake, P (1995) (2nd edition), *Spirituality and History: questions of interpretation and method*, London, SPCK.

Slee, N (1990), Parables and women's experience, in A Loades (ed.), *Feminist Theology: a reader*, London, SPCK, pp. 41–47.

Slee, N (2002), The Holy Spirit and spirituality, in S F Parsons (ed.), *The Cambridge Companion to Feminist Theology*, Cambridge, Cambridge University Press, pp. 171–189.

Smith, C M (1989), *Weaving the Sermon: preaching in a feminist perspective*, Louisville, Westminster/John Knox.

Sölle, D (1995), *Theology for Sceptics: reflections on God*, Philadelphia, Fortress.

Soskice, J M (2002), Trinity and feminism, in S F Parsons (ed.), *The Cambridge Companion to Feminist Theology*, Cambridge, Cambridge University Press, pp. 135–150.

Starhawk (1989) (2nd edition), *The Spiral Dance: a rebirth of the ancient religion of the great goddess*, New York, HarperSanFrancisco.

Stuart, E (1996), Bodiliness, in L Isherwood and D McEwan (eds), *An A to Z of Feminist Theology*, Sheffield, Sheffield Academic Press, pp. 23–24.

Tatman, L (1996), Atonement, in L Isherwood and D McEwan (eds), *An A to Z of Feminist Theology*, Sheffield, Sheffield Academic Press, pp. 10–12.

Tatman, L (2002), Western European-American Feminist Christian theologians: what might it mean to take ourselves seriously?, in C Methuen and A Berlis (eds), *The End of Liberation? Liberation in the End! Feminist theory, feminist theology and their political implications*, Leuven, Peeters Publishers, pp. 37–48.

Taylor, J V (1972), *The Go-Between God: The Holy Spirit and Christian mission*, London, SCM.

Thislethwaite, S (1990), *Sex, Race and God: Christian feminism in black and white*, London, Chapman.

Trible, P (1984), *Texts of Terror: literary-feminist readings of biblical narratives*, Philadelphia, Fortress.

Trible, P (1990), Feminist hermeneutics and biblical studies, in A Loades (ed.), *Feminist Theology: a reader*, pp. 23–29, London, SPCK.

Ward, H, Wild, J and Morley, J (eds) (1996) (2nd edition), *Celebrating Women*, London, SPCK.

Watson, N (2002), *Introducing Feminist Ecclesiology*, Sheffield, Sheffield Academic Press.

WCC (2001), *On Being Church: women's voices and visions*, Geneva, WCC.

West, A (1995), *Deadly Innocence: Feminism and the Mythology of Sin*, London, Cassell.

Willard, F (1889), *Woman in the Pulpit*, Chicago, Woman's Temperance Publishing Association.

Williams, D (1993), *Sisters in the Wilderness: the challenge of womanist God-talk*, New York, Orbis.

Woodhead, L (1999), Feminist theology – out of the ghetto?, in D F Sawyer and D M Collier (eds), *Is There a Future for Feminist Theology?*, Sheffield, Sheffield Academic Press, pp. 198–206.

Wren, B (1989), *What Language Shall I Borrow?*, London, SCM.

Young, I M (1994), Gender and seriality: thinking about women as a social collective, *Signs: a journal of women in culture and society*, 19, 710–723.

Young, P D (1995), Feminist theology from past to future, in M Joy and E K Neumaier-Dargyay (eds), *Gender, Genre and Religion*, pp. 71–82, Waterloo, Wilfrid Laurier University Press.

Zappone, K (1991), *The Hope for Wholeness: a spirituality for feminists*, Mystic, Conn., Twenty-Third Publications.

Zaru, J (2002), The demands of peace and reconciliation, *Feminist Theology*, 29, 86–95.

GLOSSARY AND BIOGRAPHY

advocacy or standpoint position a philosophical or political commitment on the side of a particular, usually oppressed, group

Althaus-Reid, Marcella contemporary queer theologian, Argentinian, working in Britain

androcentrism male-centred, the male as norm

Anselm, St (1033–1109) Italian philosopher and theologian

Augustine, St (354–430) Bishop of Hippo in North Africa

basileia the Kingdom or reign of God

beguines medieval lay women's movement

Bell, John contemporary Scottish hymn writer

Berry, Jan contemporary British feminist liturgist

Biko, Steve (1946–1977) South African nationalist leader

Brock, Rita Nakashima contemporary Asian American feminist theologian

Butler, Josephine (1828–1906) British social reformer and feminist

Butler, Judith contemporary American gender theorist

Bynum, Caroline Walker contemporary American feminist historian

Catherine of Sienna, St (1347–1380) Italian mystic and teacher of the faith

Christ, Carol contemporary American thealogian and leader of the Goddess movement

Christa a female Christ figure, usually in a crucified form

Christolatry term coined by Mary Daly to mean idolisation of Christ

Christology the study of the person and meaning of Christ

Chrysostom, John (347–407) bishop and theologian from Antioch

Clare, St (1194–1253) Italian nun and founder of Poor Clares

colonisation literally, the establishment of a colony in a country, also used metaphorically of the establishment of ownership of ideas and consciousness

Cotter, Jim contemporary British liturgist and writer

Crawford, Janet contemporary Australian feminist theologian and historian

Council of Constantinople (381) early church council which established Nicene orthodoxy

Cyril of Jerusalem (c. 315–386) Bishop of Jerusalem and theologian

dalit preferred self-designation of the so-called 'untouchable' caste in India

Daly, Mary contemporary American post-Christian radical feminist philosopher

Deane-Drummond, Celia contemporary British ecofeminist theologian

Dietrich, Gabrielle contemporary Indian feminist theologian

Douglas, Kelly Brown contemporary American womanist theologian

Dracontius (c. 450–505) African poet

D'Souza, Lucy contemporary Indian Christian artist

Duffy, Carol Ann leading contemporary British poet

dualism any view that divides reality, or some part of reality, into two opposing principles or elements, for example, mind/body

Enlightenment, the eighteenth-century 'Age of Reason', advocated 'trusting your own reason' and critical of reliance on authority and tradition

ecclesiology study of the church

ecofeminism feminist philosophy and movement committed to the liberation of the planet in tandem with women's liberation

eisegesis reading one's own meanings into rather than out of the scriptural text

enculturation the process of articulating in indigenous cultural form ideas, usually religious, from another cultural setting

epiclesis the prayer of consecration over the bread and the cup in the eucharist

essentialism, essentialist the view that particular characteristics or traits are essential to certain gender or race groups, often based on the view that biology determines such characteristics

Eusebius of Caesarea (c. 265–339) bishop and church historian, heralded as the 'father of church history'

Fiorenza, Elisabeth Schüssler contemporary German American feminist theologian

Fox, Matthew contemporary American popular theologian and leader of 'Creation Spirituality' movement

Francis of Assisi, St (1182–1226) Italian saint and mystic, founder of the Franciscan order of friars

Gandhi, Mahatma (1869–1948) Indian leader of national independence and religious teacher

gender-blind any perspective or view which does not take account of gender

gender studies the critical study of gender acquisition, development, relations and reproduction

gnostic, gnosticism loose set of groups in the second and third centuries prizing gnosis or knowledge; a religious philosophy that disparaged matter and this life, and sought escape for the soul through secret knowledge

Goddess the female principle, the female sacred deity

Goldenberg, Naomi contemporary American feminist thealogian

Grant, Jacqueline contemporary American womanist theologian

Grey, Mary contemporary British feminist theologian

Hampson, Daphne contemporary British post-Christian feminist theologian

han Korean concept meaning unrequited suffering

hegemony political rule or domination; the cultural, economic, political and social forces that ensure the domination of the ruling elite

hermeneutics literally interpretation, usually applied to texts, especially scriptural texts

hermeneutics of suspicion a critical, deconstructive method of interpretation which looks for the power bias in all theory and practice

Heyward, Carter contemporary American lesbian feminist theologian

Hildegard of Bingen (1098–1179) German mystic, theologian, musician and abbess

Hunt, Mary contemporary American lesbian feminist theologian and co-founder of WATER

Irigaray, Luce contemporary French feminist, philosopher and psychoanalyst

John of the Cross, St (1542–1591) Spanish mystic, theologian and prior

Johnson, Elizabeth contemporary American feminist theologian

Julian of Norwich (c. 1342–1420) English mystic and theologian

kenosis self-emptying, of God in the incarnation

Kristeva, Julia contemporary Bulgarian-born French feminist, philosopher and psychoanalyst

Kyung, Chung Hyung contemporary Korean feminist theologian

kyriarchy term coined by Fiorenza to signify the rule of the masters (as opposed to the rule of the fathers)

liberation theology originating in Latin America, now a global theological movement emphasising God's bias to the poor and the imperative to justice as the basis of theology

Loades, Ann contemporary British feminist theologian

Logos word or reason, the principal of order and rationality in the universe, in Christianity applied to Christ

Long, Asphodel contemporary British feminist thealogian

Lorde, Audre (1934–1992) black American feminist poet, essayist and radical activist

Lutkenhaus-Lacky, Almuth contemporary German-born Canadian sculptor

Luther, Martin (1483–1546) German Protestant Reformer

Maitland, Sara contemporary British novelist, writer and Christian feminist

Malcolm X (1925–1965) American radical black political leader

McFague, Sallie contemporary American feminist theologian

minjun Korean word meaning 'the mass of the people', the economically exploited people

misogyny hatred of women

Moltmann, Jürgen contemporary German Protestant theologian

Moltmann-Wendell, Elisabeth contemporary German feminist theologian

Morgan, Robin contemporary American feminist, writer and theorist

Morley, Janet contemporary British feminist liturgist

mujerista self-designation of American Hispanic feminist theologians

New Age wide-ranging term originating in the 1970s to refer to the belief in the arrival of the 'Age of Aquarius', now applied to many new spiritual groups and movements

Niehbuhr, Reinhold (1892–1971) American Protestant theologian

Odes of Solomon second-century Syriac liturgical texts

Oduyoye, Mercy Amba contemporary Ghanaian woman theologian

orthodoxy right belief or thought

pagan from the Latin *paganus*, meaning rural, it has been applied as a derogatory term to 'barbaric' or 'irreligious' peoples, but is now being used positively by groups who look to ancient, pre-Christian beliefs which celebrate the earth

paradigm literally, an example, pattern, model or instance, extended to a larger world-view

patriarchy literally, the rule of the fathers; the whole system which upholds male power and dominance

Plaskow, Judith contemporary American Jewish feminist theologian

pneumatology study of the Spirit

post-Christian term associated in particular with Daphne Hampson to refer to those standing within western theological tradition who have given up Christianity but remain in some dialogue with it

post-modernism extremely fluid term and movement characterised by a critique of modernity, the disappearance of the autonomous subject and the end of universal definitions, discourses and world-views

Proctor-Smith, Marjorie contemporary American feminist liturgist

praxis action for social transformation

Raphael, Melissa contemporary British Jewish feminist thealogian

Reformation sixteenth-century movement for the reform of abuses in the Roman Catholic Church, leading to the establishment of the Reformed and Protestant churches

Roberts, Michele contemporary British/French novelist and poet

Ross, Susan contemporary British feminist ecclesiologist

Ruether, Rosemary Radford contemporary American feminist theologian

Russell, Letty contemporary American feminist theologian

Saiving, Valerie contemporary American feminist theologian, whose 1960 essay on sin is often credited as the 'birth' of second-wave feminist theology

Sandys, Edwina contemporary English sculptor

second-wave feminism name given to 1960s revitalisation of the feminist movement in Europe and America, in distinction from first-wave, nineteenth-century (and earlier) feminism

sexism the expression of the basic structural injustice between the sexes in gender stereotyping of men and women as hierarchically ordered and confined to limited cultural identities and roles

Shakers nineteenth-century religious movement founded by Mother Ann Lee, so-called because of the ritual dances they performed

Söllee, Dorothee contemporary German Protestant feminist theologian and activist

Sophia wisdom, often personified as a female figure in the late Hebrew scriptures and in feminist thought

Soskice, Janet Martin contemporary British Roman Catholic feminist theologian

soteriology the study of the saving work of Christ

St Hilda Community now disbanded experimental feminist liturgical community which met in London during the late 1980s and 1990s

Starhawk contemporary American exponent of wicca and Goddess worship

stereotype standardised mental images, held by social groups, based on prejudice rather than evidence

systemic pertaining to a system or complex whole

Teresa of Avila (1515–1582) Spanish mystic and theologian

Tertullian (160–220) African theologian and apologist

thealogy, thealogian from *thea*, goddess, and *logos*, reason; the study of the Goddess

Tillich, Paul (1886–1965) German Protestant liberal theologian

Trible, Phyllis contemporary American feminist biblical scholar and theologian

WATER Women's Alliance for Theology, Ethics and Ritual, based in Silver Spring, Maryland

Watson, Natalie contemporary British feminist ecclesiologist

wicca form of neo-pagan practice and belief whose adherents usually call themselves witches

Wilberforce, William (1759–1833) British social reformer

Willard, Frances (1839–1898) American temperance and suffrage leader

Williams, Delores contemporary American womanist theologian

womanist African American feminist who claims her roots in black history, culture and religion

Womenchurch global, ecumenical movement of feminist-base communities

Wren, Brian contemporary British hymn-writer and theologian

INDEX OF THEMES

advocacy principle 7
androcentrism 4
atonement 60–71

Bible 13–24
blood, of Christ and of women 62
body, attitudes to 39–40, 64–65,
    97–98, 102
body of God 78–79

Christ, as erotic connection 57
    as saving victim 62–64
Christa 54
Christian feminism 8–9
Christology 48–59
church control of spirituality
    96–97
church, feminist theology of 83–94
church history 86–87, 91–92
church practice and ministry 84–86,
    89–90
clericalism 85–86
creation spirituality 100

dalit theology 11
death of Christ 60, 61–64, 67–69
difference in feminist theology 6–7,
    107–108
'double' oppression 10–11
dualism 3, 69–70, 97–98

ecclesiology 83–94
ecofeminism 45, 69–70
erotic 57

Eve 38–42
experience, women's 5–6, 14

female models of God 29–32, 68–69
feminist theology 1–12
    as grass-roots movement 2
    in the academy 108–109
    challenge to Christianity 115–116
    critique of 110–111
    future of 112–119
feminist spirituality 95–105

gender studies 109–110
God, models of 25–36, 76–81
Goddess movement 9, 31–32, 100
'golden thread' approach to scripture
    21–22

hermeneutics of suspicion 4
holism 104–105
Holy Spirit 53–54, 72–82

idolatry 27–28, 52

Jesus, attitudes to women 15–16,
    49–50
    as male symbol 50–51
    as liberator 55–56
    as 'scandal of particularity' 51–52
    as Sophia 56–57
    as co-sufferer, healer, provider
    57–58
    in female form 54
justice 103–104

kyriarchy 4

language, patriarchal 26–28
liberal feminism 9
liberation, in the Bible 22
liberation theology 7
liturgy, feminist 89–90

message Christologies 55–56
ministry 84–86, 92–93
minjung theology 11
mujerista theology 11
models of the church 87–88, 92
models of God 25–36, 76–81
models of holiness 97–98

parables 15–16, 22
patriarchy 4, 106–107
post-Christian feminism 9
post-modern feminism 10

racism 4, 6, 10–11
radical feminism 9–10

reading texts 'in memoriam' 20–21
recovery of neglected texts 19
redemption 60–71
relationality 33–34, 45–46, 102–103
religious language 25–36
romantic feminism 9

scripture 13–24
sexism 3–5
sin 37–47
spirituality 95–105
suffering God 62–64, 67–68
soteriology 60–71

thealogy 9
theodicy 51–52
Trinity, doctrine of 72–75, 77–79

wisdom Christologies 56–57
womanist theology 11, 57–58, 67–68
woman, views of 38–42
Womenchurch 89–90, 92–93